# Advance Praise for
## *Motivating the "What's in It for Me?" Workforce*

"The information on leading and managing generations found in this book is invaluable to all executives today. The 'war for talent' has become increasingly fierce. Attracting and retaining this talent is critical to a successful global company. This book is a masterful tool for developing the skills required for managing multigenerational teams. It is a must have for executives at all levels who are responsible for a company's greatest asset: its people."

> —Phebe Port, Vice President, Global Management
> Strategies, The Estée Lauder Companies

"*Motivating the 'What's in It for Me?' Workforce* has given our managers good ideas about leading the different generations in our workplace, particularly the New Millennials whom we at Enterprise are especially reliant upon to grow our business every single day and, ultimately, become our company's future leaders."

> —Marie Artim, Assistant Vice President, Recruiting,
> Enterprise Rent-A-Car

"After Cam presented to our management group, approximately 400 individuals, and after we responded to the clamor for his book, it became *commonplace* to hear people discussing solutions to problems based on generational considerations. There aren't many people discussions that occur today where we don't at least consider differences between Baby Boomers, Millennials, and so on. He really changed our way of thinking!"

> —Anne Donovan, U.S. Human Resources Leader,
> Systems and Process Assurance, PricewaterhouseCoopers

"If you ever had any doubt that generational differences have an impact on go-to-market strategies, Cam Marston's book, *Motivating the "What's in It for Me?" Workforce*, provides thought-provoking realities you need to consider. This is a must-read. At our Sales Leadership Conference, Cam gave our top sales managers actionable ideas on how to gain better understanding for what drives today's workforce to take direct action and deliver exceptional results."

> —Damian A. Thomas, General Manager, Corporate
> Sales Leader, General Electric Company

"Rich in insights. Far and away the most persuasive account of how to cope with the huge generational divide."

> —Amin Rajan, CEO, Centre for Research in
> Employment and Technology in Europe
> (CREATE), Pan-European Research Consultancy,
> Kent, UK

"For anyone who is interested in a positive future for his or her company or organization, this book is a must-read. Marston has helped my staff and me understand our generational differences and how to make those differences work for us, not against us."

> —Larry Naake, Executive Director,
> National Association of Counties (NACo),
> Washington, D.C.

"Understanding generational differences is changing the way we look at the world of work. Marston's insight puts him at the forefront of this thinking."

> —David Skipsey, Managing Director, Change
> Mentors, Ltd., Newcastle, UK

"This thought-provoking book is a must-read for today's manager concerned with understanding and motivating colleagues. Marston brings passion and relevance to the subject. The research is faultless, the analysis compelling, and the message clear."

> —Stephen Cowell, CEO, The Longhirst Group,
> Newcastle, UK

# MOTIVATING THE
## "What's In It for Me?"
# WORKFORCE

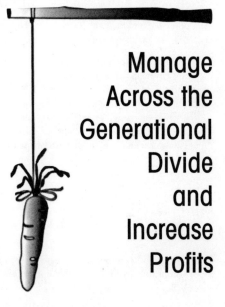

Manage
Across the
Generational
Divide
and
Increase
Profits

## CAM MARSTON

BICENTENNIAL
1807
WILEY
2007
BICENTENNIAL

John Wiley & Sons, Inc.

Published by John Wiley & Sons, Inc., Hoboken, New Jersey.
Published simultaneously in Canada.

Wiley Bicentennial Logo: Richard J. Pacifico

For general information on our other products and services or for technical
support, please contact our Customer Care Department within the United
States at (800) 762-2974, outside the United States at (317) 572-3993 or
fax (317) 572-4002.

Wiley also publishes its books in a variety of electronic formats. Some content that
appears in print may not be available in electronic books. For more information
about Wiley products, visit our web site at www.wiley.com.

*Library of Congress Cataloging-in-Publication Data:*

Marston, Cam.
    Motivating the "what's in it for me?" workforce : manage across the
generational divide and increase profits / Cam Marston.
        p.   cm.
    Includes bibliographical references and index.
    ISBN 978-0-470-12414-7 (cloth)
    1.  Employee motivation—United States.   2.  Intergenerational
relations—United States.   3.  Intergenerational communication—United
States.   4.  Supervision of employees.   I.  Title.
    HF5549.5.M63M365   2007
    658.3'14—dc22

                                                        2006036636

Printed in the United States of America.

10   9   8   7   6   5   4

*To my wife, Lisa,*
*my daughter, Reiney,*
*and my son, Spencer*

In case you're worried about what's going to become of the younger generation, it's going to grow up and start worrying about the younger generation.

—Roger Allen

Remember the generational battles 20 years ago? Remember all the screaming at the dinner table about haircuts, getting jobs, and the American dream? Well, our parents won. They're out living the American dream on some damned golf course in Vero Beach, and we're stuck with the jobs and haircuts.

—P. J. O'Rourke

The reason people blame things on previous generations is that there's only one other choice.

—Doug Larson

# Contents

# Acknowledgments

I am deeply indebted to many people whose support and assistance were noteworthy in the writing of this book.

Many, many thanks to:

Ty Boyd, Marolyn Wright, Rainey Foster, and Pat Casey for their time, ideas, encouragement, and suggestions throughout my career.

Jeanie Welch, the Business Librarian in the Reference Services Department at the University of North Carolina, Charlotte, who performed invaluable research for me and who never came up empty-handed.

The men and women I interviewed for the book, who graciously shared their experiences in the workplace with me.

My brothers, Loyd and Dale, who unwittingly were the perfect case studies and generous critics of their own managers' styles.

My father, a wise, generous, and good man. I truly hope the apple doesn't fall far from the tree.

My mother, who has been my role model and a constant source of encouragement in so many aspects of my life, especially for this book.

Larry Chilnick, who began this project with me.

Suzanne Oaks, who took a jumbled mess and created a book out of it.

And finally, Judy Knipe, who refined the manuscript and became the highlight of this entire book-writing experience.

# Introduction

## *It's Not Your Father's Workplace Anymore*

Everyone who has spent time in any workplace over the past 25 years knows that it's not like it used to be. Members of the Baby Boomer generation remember that in the post–World War II era, the 1950s, 1960s, and 1970s, there were business leaders who looked forward with burning vision. But they also knew how to look back, learn from their mistakes, and apply those lessons. Now it's the Baby Boomers who are the leaders. They, too, work hard, and many are rewarded with promotions and greater responsibilities.

But the workplace has changed, and fulfilling those responsibilities today is much tougher and more frustrating than it was for the immediate postwar generation. It's a given that no workplace is perfect and there are always job-related issues. But two new younger generations of employees, called Generation X (Gen X) and the New Millennials, have changed the workplace. These employees, many of them the same age as the Boomers' children, don't necessarily follow the traditional styles and patterns of workplace behavior. The common wisdom among Boomers is, "They aren't really interested in the future, and their vision is limited to the here and now. They don't have the seasoning or burning ambition to even want to look forward or back to learn."

On the one hand, many Boomer managers believe the concept of a work ethic will die with them; on the other, many young employees view the Boomers as dinosaurs, thanks to their limited technological ability and a shift in the demographics of the workplace itself.

Is the generational divide really that sharp and divisive? Not always—but in many companies generational issues are a common and continuing problem that can have an all-encompassing organizational impact and can lead to employee unhappiness and, ultimately, to profit loss.

## There Are Solutions

For the past eight years, I've been a lecturer and consultant for a broad range of domestic and international companies. My clients have ranged from small family-owned businesses to Fortune 500 multinational corporations. They've been headquartered both in the United States and abroad. And the audiences range from a handful of senior, top executives who are strategizing about future employee trends to groups of midlevel managers who work on a day-to-day basis with employees of all ages. I spend days preparing my research and a day on-site helping clients develop and implement new strategies—the solutions they need to get their teams to function more fluidly. All struggle with the challenges of bridging the gap between generations. Most of the company managers are Baby Boomers, while a large percentage of the workforce is now, and will increasingly be, Gen Xers and Millennials.

In the course of my work I have interviewed countless employees of every generation, and I understand the problems, values, and belief systems of each distinct generation. I know what motivates them and how they view themselves, their community, their families—and their workplaces. Their experiences in the trenches led to the insights that helped me create the solutions presented in this book—solutions that can be implemented in workplaces of every type, shape, and size.

I wrote *Motivating the "What's in It for Me?" Workforce* because I believe there is a critical need for a practical, solution-oriented reference that businesses can use to improve employee relations in the multigenerational workplace and at the same time increase profits. This book will help you discover:

- How the different viewpoints of the each generation affect the workplace.
- The basic survival skills the Boomer manager must have to cope with Gen Xers and Millennials.
- How a realistic plan with workplace-tested, concrete steps for solving the problems that may arise from generational differences can give you the freedom to explore and unlock the full potential of your organization.

Cam Marston

*Charlotte, North Carolina*
*May 2007*

# 1

## Peter Pan in the Workforce

### Pixie Dust, Forever Young, and "What Success Means to Me"

"I won't grow up / I don't want to wear a tie / And a serious expression / In the middle of July." So sang Peter Pan and the lost boys in Disney's version of the classic story. Yet to many business leaders, this childhood fantasy is being played out daily among young employees nationwide. They are an entire generation (actually two) that doesn't want to grow up. Or so it seems.

The year 2005 marked the hundredth anniversary of Sir James Barrie's *Peter Pan*. It is a fitting time to look at the role of the younger generations—specifically Generation X and the New Millennials—who today combine to make up half of the workforce, and whose values and beliefs seem to mirror those of the boy who refused to grow up. Now more than ever, Americans born since roughly 1965 do not want to follow in the footsteps of their elders. And while their managers blame it on immaturity, the reality seems to lie more in perspective. These generations do want to grow up; they just don't want to grow up to be like the generations before them.

## Time-Honored Traditions

Our nation today lives in the world created by a generation known collectively as the Matures. Born prior to 1945, they total approximately 30 million people. Heavily influenced by the military, the Mature generation created a workplace reflecting that hierarchy with a clear chain of command. Promotions, bonuses, and raises were granted when an employee (almost always a male) proved himself ready for the next level. Employees worked hard to achieve higher ranks. All employees shared a similar definition of success: climbing the company ladder and earning the rewards that came with greater responsibility. The successive job titles and associated perks were admired and envied by employees on their way up and relished by those already at the top.

This model is still the basis for a large part of today's workforce. The Baby Boomers, born between 1945 and 1964, now occupy the higher rungs of company ladders and make up 45 percent of today's workers. They are in control, but they don't always feel like it. Boomers' language of "success" and their work ethic are very similar

Each generation assumes that the succeeding generation will experience the same desires, have the same values, and appreciate and cherish the same things, in an unchanging continuum.

This hope lives on in the face of reality. I've experienced it myself with my own father, who said to me recently, "One of these days you'll realize that music gets no better than Hank Williams." What was happening? He assumed (perhaps presumed) that one of these days I'd come around to his type of music, that my tastes would mirror his, that I'd finally "get it."

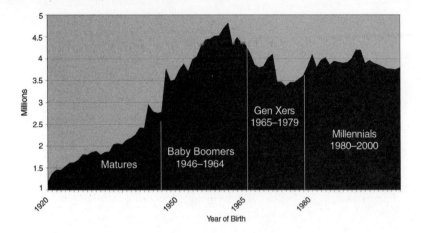

FIGURE 1.1    Today's Workplace Population by Birth Years

to those of the Matures. However, Matures now make up a mere 5 percent of the workforce. The other 50 percent—Gen Xers and the New Millennials—present a challenge to Boomer managers. (See Figure 1.1.) These younger workers are not interested in the time-honored traditions. They are unconcerned about the way things have always been done. They don't care how their managers got where they are. They are focused, often single-mindedly, on what it will take to get where they want to go.

**Generational Repetition**

Since World War II, each generation has assumed two things about the younger generations entering the workplace:

1. Senior generations assume that the younger generations will measure success the same way they themselves have.
2. Senior generations also believe that younger workers should pay their dues, following the same paths to achieve the same levels of success.

These assumptions essentially create and define the company ladder as we know it, a system that has been intact for decades in workplaces across the industrialized world. It is the apprentice-to-master relationship that has been in existence within various crafts and trades since society began. But what happens when a generation enters the workforce, learns how the senior generations measure success, and decides that it disagrees with that definition? Is this where we are today?

Gen Xers and New Millennials essentially have said to their managers—the Matures and especially the Boomers—"We don't share your definition of success. We define success differently and will pursue other rewards for our work." This change in values is having a profound impact on the work environment and on the time-honored management structure Boomers have come to rely on. The company ladder, which for generations has been the source of employee motivation, becomes irrelevant. The younger generations view their predecessors' experience as a warning, not a road map. And the traditional rules of management, motivation, and reward fly out the window.

Can this be the essence of the change going on in the workplace today? Can it be as simple, and as complicated, as a change in philosophy about the reason for working? Maybe. Time will prove this theory right or wrong. But many employers say that this is precisely what they're seeing. They describe the tremendous repercussions this change in values and principles is having on management's mode of operations—on the way executives recruit, communicate with, manage, motivate, and retain employees in order to remain competitive in the marketplace.

The newly minted attitudes and aspirations that characterize Gen X and New Millennial workers and have revolutionized the workplace are:

- A work ethic that no longer mandates a 10-hour workday.
- An easy competence in using existing and new technologies and a facility in mastering the even newer ones that appear, seemingly overnight.

- Tenuous, if not nonexistent, loyalty to any organization.
- Changed priorities for lifetime goals that can be achieved and affected by employment.

The most significant changes in perspective are in the ways older and younger generations think about time, technology, and loyalty.

## Time Is of the Essence

Time has always been a currency. But different generations value this currency in different ways. For Boomers, time has always been something to invest in the future. Boomers are working hard and putting in their time (an average 55 hours a week), and they count on a reward of some sort for their effort. Has that payout come as expected? According to the Boomers themselves, mostly not.

Gen Xers and the New Millennials regard time as something they want to control, just like their money. In fact, to them, time has an equal value to money. Many employers are coming to realize that a satisfactory trade-off, when they can't pay their younger employees more money, is to give them more time off.

Time is indeed a currency, and the younger generations are not willing to invest it in a career or a job with uncertain dividends. And in this period of job insecurity, layoffs, and changing industry, they understand that any employment is potentially unstable.

## The Technology Gap

Technology is universally recognized as critical to the success of almost any business, large or small. Smaller companies usually hire consultants or one or two employees to research, purchase, and set up new technologies to speed up work and enhance the bottom line for that particular business. In larger companies, whole departments are dedicated to the acquisition of technologies and to teaching other employees the most efficient ways to use them. Such people, the so-called techies, are usually Gen Xers and New Millennials.

Here's the problem: Matures and Boomers have grown wise over a lifetime spent in the workplace—they're looking at the larger picture. But technology *is* part of the larger picture, and confronted by even the most basic new technology, to say nothing of continuous upgrades and changes in software, and, not least, the new language developed for modern technology (techspeak), the older generations feel uneasy, threatened, and incompetent.

Meanwhile, Gen Xers and New Millennials eagerly embrace technology in its many permutations and combinations. It's not because they are more intelligent; they are simply unafraid of technology. After all, they began using computers in preschool, so to them technology has always existed. Just like indoor plumbing, electricity, and remote controls—it is a standard element of their world.

When young, technologically adept employees enter a workplace that is largely staffed by senior employees who are confused by and fearful of technology, a genuine role reversal takes place—quite a rare occurrence in our civilized world. Youth is the master, bypassing the apprentice stage altogether. Conceivably, this is one reason the dot-com bubble burst: It was created by a generation that had the technological smarts but lacked the benefits of wisdom that come from experience. The traditional workplace can become vulnerable to this scenario if the wisdom of experience doesn't exert itself. The technology gap can and must be bridged, not only for the sake of employees but for the bottom line as well.

## Loyalty

Generation X and the New Millennials have been given ample reason to question authority, not bow to it. They are skeptical of advertising and media hype; they do not automatically believe their leaders tell the truth. Repeatedly, presidents, military officials, large and small companies, and even religious institutions are caught in lies. The result is that today's younger generations almost automatically question the motives and truthfulness of institutions across the board. Ironically, the parents and leaders who established these new ground rules of distrust are the same Baby Boomers who are managing, and in conflict with, the fruits of their labors—their children.

Gen Xers and Millennials have lost their faith in institutions, both public and private, and instead have invested their loyalty and trust in individuals. Younger workers want to work for the right boss, and if they can't, they'll change jobs. The Boomers and Matures didn't have that luxury. For them, working for a disagreeable person was just part of the job description, and if you liked your boss, it was an unexpected bonus. But not liking him certainly wasn't sufficient reason to quit. For Gen Xers and New Millennials it is.

In fact, in a reversal of all that was previously held to be true and good, company loyalty is out the window, and loyalty to an individual is now the number one reason Xers and New Millennials stay at a job, especially during the first three tenuous years of employment. Dissatisfaction with the boss is the number one reason they quit. With this upheaval in values younger Americans are creating new priorities and business practices for our nation.

In the past 40 years, two other changes of enormous importance have occurred in the American workplace, one societal, the other market-driven.

## Who Is That Man in the Gray Flannel Suit?

By the late 1960s and early 1970s, the changes that were transforming American society as a whole also began to have a liberating effect on the workplace. In 1965, most employees arriving at work each morning automatically set aside their individual preferences as they crossed the threshold. An almost military conformity characterized the way the workplace operated and the way employees behaved there.

The code of behavior was embodied in numerous, mostly un-spoken, rules—a silent contract—about everything from the exact time employees began the workday to what clothing was appropriate for the job. By conforming to these rules, an employee became a so-called company man.

In the 1970s, the Boomers became a much larger population in the workforce, and the cultural and political revolution they had initiated in the 1960s began to infiltrate offices across the country. Younger workers—the Boomers—altered their uniforms a bit, veering slightly from traditional company dress codes, and they brought personal possessions into workplaces to reflect their indi-viduality. When the dot-com boom began in the mid-to-late 1990s, individual expression in the workplace had reached a peak. Young employees wore whatever they wanted to work and even brought their pets to the office with them. Companies competed for the best talent by emphasizing relaxed dress codes and encour-aging employees to decorate their work spaces in ways that would inspire them to perform.

Today, although regulations about dress have tightened some-what and free expression of style and preferences has also been tamped down, companies usually permit and, sometimes, encourage individualism. Workplaces, whether they are cubicles in a call center, executive corner offices, or nurses' stations, display their inhabitants' family, pets, hobbies, and other enthusiasms in the form of photos, screen savers, and knickknacks. Expressions of employees' tastes and preferences are alive and well in the workplace. That's the good news.

## Turmoil in the Workplace

The second sweeping change that has transformed the workplace is not so beneficial. This change does not arise from rigid and restric-tive work codes, or from misunderstandings and conflict between and among the generations. Instead, it reflects market conditions. From CEOs to service staff, from clerical workers to midlevel managers, from techies to line people, today's workplace is different from that of a decade or so ago. For many workers, whatever their jobs, the workplace seems to be in constant turmoil. For example:

- One problem is that revolving-door management is endemic. An upper-level manager in a successful international company told me he had had three presidents and two new direct bosses in one year.

- In another typical story, a manager told me that her company's very popular CEO was promoted to a newly acquired division and never replaced. The management team limped along for 11 months with the COO in charge. He, in turn, rarely left his office and canceled every management meeting the day before it was scheduled, until the division was finally disbanded and broken up, like the Soviet Union, into warring states. The COO kept his job, but the rest of the team did not.

These two examples speak to the overwhelming sense of job insecurity that has become a part of our workplace culture during the past 30 years.

Unemployment rates can be a good indicator of the health of the economy, but they don't really measure job security. In fact, there is no known measurement of job security, although there is an unofficial measurement—the number of mergers and acquisitions that have occurred in a given period.

Since 1998, there have been more than 45,000 mergers and acquisitions in which the transactions were valued at $5 million or more. Each of these actions has had ripple effects. Companies merge, and very often workers are let go when their jobs become redundant. The executives I've talked with don't simply blame poor upper management or Enron-style corruption, which are unusual and far outside the norm. These leaders see a consistent corporate culture that has not evolved to meet the new demands of the workplace and employees today.

### In Search of Pixie Dust

In the Barrie play, Peter Pan sprinkled pixie dust over the children so they could fly with him to Neverland. There, they would remain young forever, free from grown-up rules and responsibilities. There is no pixie dust. All of us understand that, even Gen Xers and New Millennials. But these two generations do want to live their youthful years, as much as possible, on their own terms, following their individual paths to their personal concepts of success.

So what will it take to harness the skills of a multigenerational workforce? What are today's requirements for leading young people who see Baby Boomers as outdated and out of touch? It will take:

- A new understanding of what employees want from their jobs, their bosses, and their workplace experience.
- A new understanding of loyalty—how the word has changed, why it changed, and why pay, benefits, and opportunities for promotion are not nearly as important in creating job loyalty as they used to be.
- A new definition of "self"—that young employees today define themselves by who they are outside the job, not by what they do for a living, which is a departure from senior generations.
- A new behavior from leaders in the workplace who must realize that younger generations enter the workplace seeking self-fulfillment from the get-go and aren't interested in paying their dues for an unknown period of time.
- A new comprehension that youth today remain in their youth much longer than ever before, being able to live at home longer, stay in school longer, get married later, and have children later, which dramatically affects their commitment to their workplace.

Because these younger generations are already approximately 50 percent of the nation's employees, right now the condition of the workforce landscape is still uncertain. But rest assured that this is not the first time one (usually older) generation has looked upon another and been concerned for the future. Aristotle complained about the ethics and behaviors of the younger generations. Peter Pan challenged his elders at the turn of the twentieth century. Society has been here before. We'll be here again.

And, ultimately, it will all work out. But one thing is certain: The changes in business outlook and policies that today's younger generations are experiencing are real and will continue to affect us all. As the manager of a small firm, a midlevel vice president of a local corporation, or an executive of a large company, you are concerned about your ability to attract and keep employees—some of whom are also your potential customers, of course.

This is the right time for another change in the way businesses are run and how they function. The generational divide that now separates the Boomers from Gen Xers and Millennials may look unbridgeable. On one side are the Boomers, an entrenched group with 30 years of workplace experience—often with only one or two companies. They are used to doing everything their way.

On the other side of the divide is an increasingly large, skittish group of employees who have entered the workplace with college diplomas, superior technical skills, a different life strategy from that of their predecessors, and little regard for the establishment.

The gap can be bridged. To avoid havoc and to improve your bottom line, you can and must learn to make the adjustments recommended in this book. These changes are necessary if you are to get the most from—and give the most to—this vast new population of employees.

There is no magic pixie dust that will make these generations "grow up and come to their senses." Anyone waiting for that ought to grab a chair and get really comfortable. Yes, some generational differences reflect the desire and will of each new generation to change the world, at least its surface styles and attitudes. However, other differences speak to the heart of these generations' personal goals. The challenge is to determine which differences are superficial and which are deeply held convictions—and to reconcile those convictions with the traditional workforce hierarchy model. In the end, there is no Neverland to escape to; we must all make an effort to understand each generation and determine the best way to define success in the current workforce environment.

# 2

## The Boomers and Matures

### *There They Go.*
### *Wait, Maybe Not!*

Conventional wisdom goes that most retirees want to settle in a nice retirement community, play golf, do some volunteer work, and putter around the garden. Most of the Matures are retiring, and a lot of them actually pursue just such a relaxed lifestyle. But there are also a great many older workers who choose to remain in their jobs. Some are executives who have reached upper management positions and are unwilling to give up the good salaries, benefits, recognition, and prestige that go along with executive life. They may have enough money to carry them through the rest of their lives, but they cannot imagine what they will do without a job as an anchor. They fear retirement as the great unknown.

Others, when forced to retire, choose to enter new fields because they still need a steady income. They start consulting businesses, or become teachers or administrators; they take courses to upgrade their technical skills. Their lifetime guarantee has expired too soon. The money for retirement has not been enough for them to live on; unexpected health problems linked to a prolonged life span may arise that are not adequately covered by private insurance or Medicare.

Even so, most employees in any business do expect to retire at some point. But early retirement or an arbitrary cutoff age for older workers can produce a rarely recognized economic effect on the businesses they leave. When these employees leave their jobs, they no longer can pass along their experience and management skills to newer workers, and a company's resources may be weakened.

The Matures, known popularly as the Greatest Generation, were born before 1945. They witnessed the dawn of the nuclear age. They fought in World War II and Korea. They built the United States into the superpower it is today. Driven by the need to win the Cold War and escape The Bomb, the Matures became more successful than any previous generation of Americans.

The Matures also spearheaded development of the technology that Boomers later improved to open up even greater opportunities for those entering the workplace. (And those newer employees themselves are upgrading the technology to the point where the Boomers are having problems keeping up.)

## We *Say* We Want a Revolution

Matures regarded Boomers as the generation to whom they could eventually turn over the reins, the generation that would ensure continuity and would maintain flourishing businesses. That is not exactly the way it turned out.

Yes, the Boomers wanted that inheritance—the titles, the equity, and the security that their parents' generation had fought for. For decades, it looked as if this scenario would play out well. However, the story has taken an unexpected turn.

The Baby Boomers brought something totally new with them when they began arriving in the workplace. The United States was in turmoil, the Vietnam War was at its height, and dissension and protest were common at college campuses and elsewhere across the country. Minority groups were demanding, and beginning to achieve, equal opportunity.

The counterculture was a *happening thing, baby*, and it affected everyone, whatever their values. Some of the Boomers' mantras were: "Make love, not war," "Don't trust anyone over 30," and "Hell no, we won't go." No one had seen anything like it—a whole generation that cherished nonconformity and declared themselves free to pursue it, in opposition to the so-called silent generation of the 1950s, both at home and in the workplace.

The Boomers, however, despite their shaggy looks and laid-back style, were very well educated and conscious of their goals. It was good news for the economy that this very large generation of workers, however nonconformist, was also highly motivated toward success. Many of them had advanced degrees and technical training, and they were eager to prove themselves in the workplace.

How did these so-called Baby Boomers view their bosses? Even if you hadn't marched on Washington or protested the Vietnam War, you thought these "suits" were still the establishment because they were over 30. They were not to be trusted. They were the generation who had been buttoned down at work since the 1950s. The only rebels in their crowd were on TV—Maynard G. Krebbs and Dobie Gillis!

As the war in Vietnam wound down, profound social changes were integrated into our lives—the early stirrings of feminism, minority quotas, more relaxed dress codes, and the great surge in

In 1946, 2.8 million children were born, and about 20 years later this population entered the workforce. In 1947, 3.8 million children were born—1 million more than the previous year. In 1955, 4.3 million children were born, and the number remained at about this level for each of the next five years. This surging population became the workforce from which the Matures selected their staffs.

technological applications, to mention only a few. The workforce evolved, too. Professional, highly educated working mothers, for example, became more common, which changed the workplace forever. Sex, drugs, and rock 'n' roll lost their luster in the 1980s, or as soon as the Baby Boomers realized that babies required diapers and houses required mortgage payments. They were loath to admit it, but many felt they were selling out their ideals. The conflict Boomers are now experiencing in the workplace is that when they see the next generations of workers—Gen Xers and New

*The Big Chill* was one of the most popular movies aimed at the Baby Boomers. The 1983 film follows an impromptu, postfuneral reunion of several Baby Boomer friends who went to school together in the 1960s. Two are married, and others are working their way up the professional ladder or looking for ways to make even more money in the entertainment industry.

The film explores their memories, dreams ("Remember the land we were going to get for the commune?"), and their feelings about the good old days—12 years before. One story line focuses on the ticking biological clock of a successful female lawyer. For another, the question is whether to sell a successful home-grown business to a large company. The others are struggling with personal growth. All of this is set in an affluent location, a coastal resort in South Carolina. The young cast, all of whom became major stars, epitomized the Baby Boomers' new version of the American dream: "You can have your cake and eat it, too." The film is now a classic because most Baby Boomers identified with the conflicts experienced by the characters. However, in the end, the characters all returned to their normal lives, as did the audience.

Millennials—they don't see anyone that vaguely resembles who they were in their own youth when they entered the workforce. But they do see who they, themselves, *have become* every morning when they look in the mirror.

Most demographers believe that what people experience between the ages of 14 and their mid-20s will stick with them and make them who they are for the rest of their lives. Although people don't remain static after that, many of their values have already been set—shared values that create, bond, and define a generation. An obvious example of this is anyone who has firsthand experience of the Great Depression. It is seldom that you come across an individual who survived the Depression who is a spendthrift or wasteful in other ways.

## The Struggles of Two Generations

Who the Mature and Boomer generations are can be seen in my own family history, which, like that of so many other American families, illustrates the hardships, job experiences, living arrangements, education, expectations, culture, and values of the four generations working so uncomfortably together today.

### *Matures: A Way of Life*

By the time my grandmother died at 92 years of age, she had seen a lot. She rarely left Mobile, Alabama, the city she moved to as a young girl, where she married and raised her four boys, but from that city she was able to watch her world change around her.

Several months before she died, I sat with her and listened as she remembered where she came from and how she lived, stories I had never heard before. It became clear to me, as she talked, how differently her generation and mine saw the world.

I remember getting into a little debate with her one day by challenging her to define her generation in one word. What one overriding characteristic defined her generation? What one word summed it up?

Without hesitation she said, "Sacrifice. My generation knows sacrifice. We lived through it as children, then as young adults, and we can handle it better today than anyone else. We know sacrifice."

"Sacrifice?" I said, playing up my role as her opponent in this debate. "I know sacrifice. My peers know sacrifice. We use the word regularly to apply to our own situations. How can you say your generation should claim that word?"

She knew that the best way to defend her answer was to tell me about her life. She began this way:

"I remember being hungry as a child. My father was a preacher and we lived in Mississippi. He traveled to find places that would let him preach and he'd take any money the congregation would give him. There were times when there wasn't much money for us." She paused and looked at me. "Have you ever been hungry?" she asked, "and you didn't know where your next meal would come from?"

I just shook my head. The truth is I've never had to worry about the basics of life.

"I remember the clothes I wore as a girl," she continued. "I didn't have much to choose from, of course. I remember getting a simple white dress that I would wear to Sunday services. I thought I looked so pretty in it. But as young people do, I grew. And it wasn't too long before I had outgrown that dress. But my parents didn't have enough money to buy me a new one, so I wore that dress every Sunday for something like three years. I remember being embarrassed to wear that dress when it became obvious I had long outgrown it, but I had nothing else to wear to church." Again she looked at me to see if there was anything I had experienced that could relate to her story.

I shook my head.

"When I met your grandfather the [Second World] War was on its way. We had just been married when it started. Right around a year later your grandfather left to do his part. I remember the day he left. We had moved in with his parents after we married and lived in a small spare bedroom. The day he left for the services, I stood on the front steps of my mother-in-law's house with my first-born son in my arms. This would be your father, of course. He was only a handful of months old at the time, if that. Your grandfather left us and rounded the street corner to catch the bus that would take him off to war. As I stood there with that baby that day I wondered to myself, 'Will I ever see him again?' There were people on our street, sons and husbands, that weren't coming home.

"Have you ever wondered if you'd ever see a loved one again, knowing that they were heading off to a war where you know people that have been killed?"

Again I shook my head. "No," I said.

"During the war years in the summer I'd sit out on the front porch of my mother-in-law's house after working all morning cleaning and cooking. I remember having two children now. Your father was old enough to get around on his own, but not old enough for us to let him roam without us watching. His brother, your uncle, was born while his father was stationed in Guam. On the front porch we'd fan ourselves to try to beat the heat. This is long before anyone had air-conditioning, mind you. And as we sat on the porch we'd talk to our neighbors who were outside fanning themselves just like we were. We could hear the chatter of the neighbors up and down the block as they all took a break during the hottest part of the day and caught up on the gossip and the news as they chatted from porch to porch.

"Every now and then we'd notice the conversation at the end of the street stop. We knew exactly what was happening. We'd turn and watch a serviceman slowly drive down the street as he looked for a specific street number and we'd pray that he'd keep going, that he'd pass us by. There wasn't a word spoken by anyone. When he found the house he was looking for, he'd stop his car in front, and we would hear the mother or wife or both begin crying. We all knew that he was delivering a telegram saying that their son or husband had been killed, and we'd gather our children and rush to their house to do anything we could to console them. We knew that the next time it could be us.

"From time to time a letter would arrive from your grandfather recounting where he was and what he was doing. Some would tell me that he'd be in port for a short time and that I should come visit him with the children. He was in the Navy and his ship would pull into San Diego. When I learned that he was going to be in port, I immediately began planning to go see him and would drive from Mobile to San Diego with two children under five years old in the car. Keep in mind," she said, "that this is before air conditioning, before the interstate highway system. We had to ration gas, and the maximum speed limit during wartime was 35 miles per hour. And I made the trip twice in the four years he was away.

"And when he finally returned from the war we had to start all over again. His dental practice had stopped while he was away and he had to begin finding new clients, since his old ones had found new dentists. It was hard for a long time after the war, too.

"Before the war was the Depression, and there wasn't much to be had by anyone," she said. "During the war was rationing and our husbands and fathers were away; many of them never came back. And after the war we had to start back at zero again. It was hard. We learned to value the little that we had. And we learned that sacrifice was a way of life. My generation knows sacrifice."

When she finished, I conceded that her generation deserved to use the word *sacrifice* to describe themselves. The experiences of the Depression and World War II stuck with her and influenced her behavior daily, even in her nineties when the world had changed around her dramatically. My grandmother and her entire generation lived through the hardest times that then became boom times. Yet it was the hardest times that had the most lasting impact. The boom times were fun, but the hard times made them who they are.

My peers and I have never known war as my grandmother had. Some of my peers served in the Gulf War, and others have fought in

Afghanistan, but we have never known a global war like World War II—either on the battlefront or left at home, hoping, praying, and living with ration cards for everything from butter to shoes to gasoline. We know nothing about living through a massive, nationwide Depression. We've gone through a few recessions, but we have never experienced my grandmother's level of struggle.

## Boomers: A Way of Work

With my grandmother's defense of her generation's sacrifice fresh in my mind, I went to my mother, a Baby Boomer. "Mom," I said, "if you were asked what sacrifices you had to make in your life thus far, what comes to mind?"

"Work," she said without hesitation. "I had to make big sacrifices for work. For my generation and me, we had to give a lot to our jobs. We had to sacrifice family, friends. We had to sacrifice the time we wanted to spend with our children to be at work. We were the original workaholics. We thought that the longer and harder you worked the more successful you'd be. We also had to fight to keep our jobs a number of times due to recessions and downsizing, and the way we fought was to show our bosses that we worked longer and harder than the next person. We sacrificed a lot for our work."

These two definitions of sacrifice are completely different. Both tell what each generation had to do to make it. And these stories, I've learned since, are typical for Matures and Boomers.

Comparatively, what do my generation (Gen Xers) and the generation following me (New Millennials), know about sacrifice? Can we relate? Do we have similar experiences to share? Not really. The vast majority of us have not had to give up very much. We have no clue what it is like to be hungry, nor have we lived though a world war. We sympathize deeply with the tragic, agonizing loss suffered by families of soldiers who have died or been wounded in the Middle East conflict, but we still believe that it is, at least for the present, a limited war, not one that will engulf almost every family in the nation.

As for the economy, recently it has taken a downturn, but I'm not aware of anyone who has resorted to workaholism to fight for his or her job. It may happen someday but, to my knowledge, it hasn't happened yet.

The events that shaped my grandmother and my mother are the filters through which they look—filters that color the world these women see, filters that have created a value system to use in judging others. I know that if my grandmother were to see me throw away a Ziploc bag after one use, she would accuse me of being wasteful. But I am oblivious because I've grown up in a world of disposable items: pens, cameras, diapers, bottles of water, coffee prepackaged in a filter, toner cartridges, with still more to come. To me, the Ziploc bag is *designed* to be thrown away after one use.

Most people born in the same generation have very similar attitudes and value systems that they acquire while they are young and that remain with them throughout their lives. The various generational characteristics discussed in this book will probably apply to most people you know in each generation, but they won't apply to everyone in a generation.

Many factors go into making up an individual, and generational preferences and biases are only one part of them. There are many psychological profiling systems that businesses can purchase for categorizing their employees (DiSC and Myers-Briggs being two of the most popular), but the systems can't perfectly predict all of a person's behaviors, and the generational characteristics don't describe every person or every aspect of that person. Family affluence, birth order, new immigrant or native-born, childhood work experience, and numerous other factors combine to make each person an individual. Again, their generation is only a piece of the puzzle.

The Matures, relying on military models, created the workplace that is still in place today. It has been altered a bit since its creation, but it still largely reflects the same workplace created immediately following the World War II. And there is no denying that it was and still is a very effective model. The United States is the last remaining superpower, and that is a testament to the vision and energy that the Mature generation contributed to our society—their innovation, work ethic, discipline, focus, concept of a clear chain of command, and other excellent qualities. From the time they returned home as the victors in a world war, they created a playing field from which all of us have benefited.

## Generational Voices

Recently, as I wrote this book, I conducted a series of interviews with workers across the United States. They told me how their lives have been affected by the multigenerational aspects of the workplace. Their disparate experiences in the trenches helped me form the basic advice in this book. Each person's story is different, but there are also commonalties, which can contribute to some solutions to intergenerational issues.

*Subject:* **Wofford O'Sullivan**
*Age:* **51**
*Location:* **Columbia, South Carolina**
*Title:* **Education Associate, Office of Career and Technology Education**
*Employer:* **South Carolina State Department of Education**

*Cam Marston: Tell me about your background.*

*Wofford O'Sullivan:* We had a positive outlook. As I thought back through my elementary, junior high, and high school years, and even beyond that, it occurred to me that I always grew up in a community that promoted a lot of the good things in life.

In talking with my two sons, I think if any part of that attitude or idealism has changed it is that today our lives are tempered with death like we dealt with on September 11. It is right in the forefront of our thinking. But even prior to that, taking that event away, there's still a lot of negative stuff in the headlines every day. My sons have access to computer technology, e-mail, and all the magazines and newspaper headlines. They have a lot of information coming their way. When I was growing up, I'm sure all that information was there and available but it did not seem to be highlighted. The positive things, the work ethic, the America moving forward are what I remember.

*C.M.: Where do you think that attitude came from? That positive work ethic, America moving forward, et cetera.*

*W.O'S.:* I would go back to my father's generation and probably to his father's generation, when so much of the fundamental basis for knowledge that we have today was developed. It wasn't just the country and rural scenario, but people all across America, in the more populated areas and in the more rural areas, really had to depend upon each other. There was a team feeling. It was a neighbor-help-neighbor, team-oriented effort, just to survive. Not to have extraordinary riches or all the real niceties of life, but just to survive. That has a lot to do with it.

*C.M.: Has the media created this change?*

*W.O'S.:* I have a problem with media, because I think that they do create a lot of the negativism. I try to be objective, but they have a job to do—to present the news. They print what they know the public is going to read and pay for. I buy the *Spartanburg Herald Journal*. I know what the headlines are going to be most of the time. Or I can go online and get it. What I remember is people reaching for, grasping for, and holding on to the positive. Now I see people not reaching for and grasping the negative, but they're really selling newspapers today, if you know what I'm saying.

*C.M.: When you think of the workplace here, what pumps you up? What makes you want to work hard?*

*W.O'S.:* No doubt—a pat on the back, and it doesn't even have to be that, really. Sometimes a smile, but a pat on the back and somebody telling me I'm doing a good job.

*C.M.: Just the word of mouth.*

*W.O'S.:* I don't think there's any doubt in my mind for my generation [Boomers]. I've actually talked with other people here in the office of my generation, and there's no doubt about that response.

*C.M.: So title, dollars, public recognition . . . all come well below?*

*W.O'S.:* It's definitely below someone telling me I've done a good job: "Wofford, that program was really well organized," or "Wofford, I really appreciated that content you delivered." Oh yeah, absolutely.

*C.M.: What are the differences in the generations? What have you seen that's different?*

*W.O'S.:* Well, I've already seen it in talking with some peers here and with my son who is graduating from Clemson next year. He's worked hard, gotten good grades, all those things. I think that, bless their hearts, both my sons, in some ways I've failed them. I think maybe members of my generation have all failed our children by making things too easily accessible and by providing them with things up front without having them develop a really strong work ethic. But my son talks in terms of job hunting for dollars only. The money has been there; the things, the stuff that he has needed has been there. He's intelligent enough to know that it has taken money, so when he thinks of success for himself he has to have money. He'll want to try to do a good job, but the motivating thing for him, when he decides who he's going to interview with, is annual salary.

*C.M.: Do you think that will change or is that a part of him that's always going to be there?*

*W.O'S.:* I think it's a part of his generation that's going to be there.

*C.M.: How do you celebrate successes at work?*

*W.O'S.:* That is an interesting question. A lot of times we celebrate success just by getting together as a group or as a team, reviewing a successful program, pointing out strengths and weaknesses, just getting together and . . . how can I say it . . . basking in the glow of success—not in terms of monetary success, but in delivery of a program or information or an initiative.

*C.M.: Do you have an event in mind that reflects that?*

*W.O'S.:* We have an event here, in the building in the State Department of Education, where initiatives are celebrated. We have food—somebody may put together a covered dish. We say, "Hey, we had a great summit last year. When we get back we're going to have a covered dish. We're going to celebrate that and talk about it, the pluses and minuses."

*C.M.: Who are the heroes for your age group?*

*W.O'S.:* That is a tough one for me. Colin Powell just kind of jumps to mind: the Desert Storm thing. I think Colin Powell is the one that I claim as a hero of my generation.

*C.M.: How about stereotypes of your generation? Are there any that are correct? Incorrect? Do you fit any of them?*

*W.O'S.:* If my generation is stereotyped, it is a work ethic–oriented stereotype. I work hard. I was taught to work hard; I remember that very, very vividly from my parents. I learned really early, on a

60-acre farm and on the back of a trash truck. I know what a 12- and 15-hour workday is. I was taught the value of work. So, if part of that stereotype is work orientation and work ethic, then I fit that stereotype.

*C.M.: Define work ethic a bit more.*

*W.O'S.:* It's more than amount—it's quality. Quantity and quality. I think quality is probably the more significant of those two. But it's a consistency—there every day, there on time, knowing what needs to be done, doing it without having been told to do it, with the expectation that there won't be a thank-you, a pat on the back, whatever. I think I'm correct in saying this for my generation.

*C.M.: Your peers would agree?*

*W.O'S.:* We expect it from each other. I think my generation really desires to fit into whatever work environment we find ourselves in. We tend to be pretty tough on those who don't fit.

*C.M.: If you could prioritize what creates fit, work ethic would be way up there. What else?*

*W.O'S.:* Teaming. To me, that is something that's carried through our generation. I grew up where a man would drive two miles through the country and sit on a neighbor's front porch for an afternoon and say, "Bring your mules over to my farm and let's plow this cotton together." That whole attitude of survival then has transferred to the workplace today. *Fit* means willingness to share resources and being willing to be a part of the whole picture.

*C.M.: When someone doesn't fit, what is it that makes them a poor fit?*

*W.O'S.:* The first thing that comes to my mind is ego: if they're in it for a spotlight for themselves. They want to be among those listed when the whole thing is over, but they might not have pitched in the way they should have. They're a member of the team that just didn't get their part of the work done.

*C.M.: Can you recall something specific that someone may have done that you disliked—something that told you, "I'm not going to work well with this individual"?*

*W.O'S.:* Yeah. The "I" trouble. I need to do this. . . . I need to show you how to do that. . . .

*C.M.: Has your generation lived up to your expectations?*

*W.O'S.:* I don't know that at any point I actually even thought through what I expected of my generation. I remember back to a su-perlative that we gave in high school—*Most Likely to Succeed.* It was a superlative that I received, but it goes back to the definition of suc-cess. I think I read somewhere that my son's generation is the first in many generations that will actually not have it better than their par-ents. That's interesting to me. So, if I had to come up with a "yes" or "no," I would probably say "no" on the basis of that information. I feel that if we'd met our expectations and been totally successful in whatever ways there may have been to be successful, our sons' gener-ation would have it better than we have it.

*C.M.: What is your definition of success?*

*W.O'S.:* It is being comfortable. It's not only a success oriented to-ward money, but a success oriented toward being comfortable, to-ward being happy: getting up every morning and knowing the importance of enjoying what you do, day in and day out. In addition to that, a big part of that is family oriented. At least I think so.

*C.M.: What are the steps to becoming successful?*

*W.O'S.:* Education, hard work, and priorities in terms of family and community and the needs of other people, I think.

*C.M.: When you remember the good times, what are they?*

*W.O'S.:* We only had about 60 acres of land when I was growing up, at least for my teenage years, and we ended up selling that. I think my dad only finished the third grade. We taught him to sign his name. But he became the most successful businessman, and it had nothing to do with education. My dad had more common sense probably than most people I've ever known in my life. He didn't have much education, but he sold that farm and went into the sanitation, garbage business. He became extremely successful with less than a third grade education because he was willing to "beat the sun in the sky" and he was willing to "go in with the moon," and to do everything it took in between those times, all those long hours, to provide service to the people he was working with.

We would come out of the cotton field—we'd have about 15 acres of cotton—and he'd always give us Saturday afternoon off. He knew we wanted to get a bath (and we had to take a bath every day—it was not one of those once-a-Saturday things). But we'd get our bath and Dad would take us somewhere, usually just riding in the country or to go get a haircut, and then he'd take us somewhere for a meal that evening. That's one of the things that jumps out for me. There's probably thousands more but, boy, those were the good times for me. We loved it. . . . We loved that part of our lives.

*C.M.: How do you want your generation remembered, Wofford? I assume you consider yourself a Boomer?*

*W.O'S.:* Yeah. I don't know. I think in some ways I'm very much like everyone else in the Boomer generation, and in some ways I may be radically different. I don't know; I think I would like my generation remembered as a generation that became a little more appreciative of other cultures—a generation that appreciated knowledge but a generation that never lost touch with the essence of a human being. I guess that's the best way I can say it.

*Subject:* Anonymous
*Age:* Boomer
*Location:* Syracuse, New York
*Occupation:* Fund-raising for a nonprofit job-skills training
     organization

*Cam Marston: What are your generation's overall concerns today?*

*Anonymous:* We're afraid of getting older. The ads say you have to stay young. Everyone is afraid of getting older more than anything else. The state of the stock market right now doesn't help.

*C.M.: What is their attitude toward work today?*

*Anon.:* Everyone must work. Their 401(k)s are eaten by the stock market. College is expensive. Divorce is rampant. You have no value if you don't work. Work is important. What you do is important.

*C.M.: What incentives work with your generation?*

*Anon.:* Money. Toys. Cars. Fame.

*C.M.: When you look at someone and think, "Wow, that person is very successful," what are you seeing when you say that?*

*Anon.:* People who have been able to hold a marriage together. Whose kids have turned out okay. Who accept themselves the way they are. Who're realistic. Who you can have a real talk with. We're all jealous of people who have managed to hold things together when the rest of us couldn't. People who have lost things through divorce or through the stock market and have realized that things don't make you happy. It is the internal things that make you happy and we're all recognizing that now.

*C.M.: What incentives do you want in order to get a job done well?*

*Anon.:* Since I am in a job where I control my schedule, I have all the time off I need. Right now if I were offered an incentive I'd want it to be monetary. If I had a regular job, I'd want it to be time off.

*C.M.: Do you ever change the way you speak or the language that you use when dealing with members of different generations?*

*Anon.:* Yes. With people my age we can talk forever about health—my health, their health, et cetera. People younger than me don't want to talk about health. And they don't want to hear that people are dying. They don't want to be scared. They're afraid enough when their kids are running a fever or have the measles or something.

*C.M.: Do you expect people of different ages to speak to you differently because of the age differences?*

*Anon.:* No, and I hate when they do that because it's just another reminder that I don't fit in with their group and that they view me as an outsider. I like it when a whole group works together and they forget about ages and gender and color and things like that. It is hard to do without reaching a consensus unless you have a real dedication to a cause.

*C.M.: How do you celebrate success at work?*

*Anon.:* I bring my employees a brownie. Or candy. I congratulate them and write up a memo. I make sure everyone knows when they've completed an event successfully. I'll rewrite their resume to show that they now know how to do this. It makes them happy. It is interesting. They didn't realize what running an event would do for them. They were put in the program as the organizer, and they get the credit as the one that pulled it off.

*C.M.: So celebrating success has a lot to do with letting a lot of people know who's done well. Is that correct?*

*Anon.:* Yes. I make their job into more than just their job description, not in terms of just more work but in terms of more skills and more positive feedback.

*C.M.: Do you like it when that is done for you when you've had success?*

*Anon.:* Absolutely. Absolutely.

*C.M.: What are the biggest stereotypes of the Baby Boomers?*

*Anon.:* Well, we still have a lot of stereotypes about race. It's coming out more as people get older. They were clever enough to not let it out when they were young, but now it's beginning to emerge. I hear a lot more racist comments that people wouldn't dare to say several years ago. Maybe it's a result of 9/11 somehow. It is mainly in my age group, too. It is certainly not in the age groups under me. What was hidden is coming out.

*C.M.: Are there any stereotypes that fit the Baby Boomers?*

*Anon.:* I think that people are beginning to realize that everything can be negotiated. They didn't know that before.

*C.M.: What is the best way you've learned to administer a reprimand to an employee?*

*Anon.:* I try to emphasize the way I felt. I ask them for any input they may have into the whole thing. I try to interject a little humor into it. The best way I've learned to deliver a reprimand is the way I'd want it done to me. Give it immediately, don't pout, and don't put anyone in the corner. Allow them a way to get out of it while maintaining some dignity.

*C.M.: Is it ever appropriate to go around your boss for something?*

*Anon.:* Hell, yes! It's the only way. The fearless leader who can't handle people going around him is not really a fearless leader.

*C.M.: Is it important to you to fit in at your office?*

*Anon.:* Yes. To me it means that when you take a job you observe the traditions and the values and the icons and the other things that are important to people. You observe things before you try to change them. You make sure these things are not in place for reasons that you don't understand. Once people understand that you're there to become a part of the group and you're not there to change or criticize or threaten them, you become part of them. It's very important.

It's important to come in and say "Hello" to them and ask some questions to let them know you want to know what's going on with them. You're with them eight to ten hours a day, and they do become your family. Fitting in is essential.

*C.M.: And what happens to those that don't fit in?*

*Anon.:* They quit. Generation X came into their jobs wanting to change things rapidly. But they were frustrated. They didn't realize how slow some things are to change. Then they felt too distant and they felt they had to leave. You'd later learn that they had left someplace before you and some other place before that and on and on.

*C.M.: What makes you like someone you work with?*

*Anon.:* I can't think of anyone I don't like. I think people are very interesting even if they're a pain in the butt. Generally, when you spend a little time thinking about it, you can realize where they're coming from. But the people I really like are the ones who have a good sense of humor, who like what they're doing.

*C.M.: What is your generation most concerned about?*

*Anon.:* Money: not having enough—for college, for kids, taking care of aging parents, so we can stay in our big houses, and so that we can live to be a hundred.

*C.M.: What are the steps necessary to becoming successful?*

*Anon.:* You have to be very adaptable.

# 3

# Up, Up, and Awaaaaay!

## *The Boomers Soar at Work*

So many Baby Boomers were born immediately after World War II that there were scarcely enough hospitals to hold them. Children in grade school sat on windowsills because classrooms had too few desks. Staggering numbers of kids overran the schools, nurseries, and businesses catering to children.

The kids grew up and, by their very numbers, they had a powerful, electrifying effect on the workplace. Boomers began working in a business world that had been retooled (literally and figuratively) by the Matures, and they made it soar. It was as if the Matures created a

- In 1970, the Baby Boomer generation stretched from 6 to 24 years old. At that time, the number of people between the ages of 25 and 44 was 48 million.

- In 1990, when the Baby Boomers were between the ages of 26 and 44, their population was almost 81 million—closing in on double the previous generation's size.

nice, reliable automobile that was the U.S. economy after World War II. The car ran smoothly, was dependable, and required little attention. Then the Boomers added a turbocharger, and the economy began rocketing off the charts.

Along with the expanded workforce, three other factors have transformed the business community that the Boomers entered and eventually took over, a community that is now being passed along to Gen X. These factors are a new work ethic, the counterculture in command, and newer and fewer jobs.

## A New Work Ethic

When the Matures hired the Boomers, they said, "Congratulations. You have a job here. The company thinks you'll be a good fit. We hope you'll do well and make this organization proud. You'll need to follow the rules, learn to fit in, and stay in line. Good luck."

The Matures rarely used "I" or "me" in the workplace; it was always "the company" and "we." And to do well you had to "learn to fit in and stay in line." The message was simple: "There are many more of you out there, and we'll be happy to find someone else to replace you if you don't work out." To hold on to those jobs and get ahead of their peers, the Boomers began competing with one another boldly and openly—behavior rarely seen before in the workplace.

With the playing field level in terms of skills and education, the Boomers realized that the most direct path to the top could be found by working long and working hard. And they excelled at long, hard work. In fact, no single generation had ever before put in so many hours with so much intensity, and a new term, *workaholic*, was coined in the 1970s to describe these work habits.

For the Boomers, hard work began to equate to time spent at the job. Eventually a person's work ethic (read *value*) was equated to the number of hours he or she spent working on a daily or weekly basis.

My uncle entered this workplace, and after several years of working hard for his company he decided he couldn't do it anymore. He resigned and delivered his resignation personally to all those he needed to speak with. In planning when he would tell them, he decided to do it on a day he knew everyone would be in the office—Sunday.

Ask Boomers, even today, if they have a strong work ethic, and their response will be something like, "Absolutely. I work 50 hours a week at the very minimum." It's a badge of courage or a boast.

The Boomers' work ethic came to define their lives. At first it defined how much money they would make. Their line of thinking was simple: The longer they worked, the more they would be paid. To beat out their office peers in the competition for raises, bonuses, and promotions, Boomers worked longer and harder. They spent so much time at work, they'd joke with one another that they commuted home, not to work.

## Visible Workers, Visible Rewards

It was important for employees to be seen working hard at their desks—it was visible time. Output was not measured nearly as much as hours spent working. Working from home didn't count, and if you came in on Saturday it didn't count, either, unless someone, preferably the boss, saw you there. What you actually accomplished on Saturday was less important than your presence on the job.

All of this was quite predictable; it simply followed the laws of supply and demand. The Boomers—as a surplus quantity of supply—had to distinguish themselves with something in order to be chosen. Thus, their work ethic became the field of battle.

That work ethic reflects Boomers' personal sense of self-worth. They know they have value because they work so hard and so long. The competitive mode that the Boomers engaged in early in their careers still guides many of them today.

When they win, when their work ethic is superior and they've defeated their peers, when they've been given the raise, bonus, or promotion—they want their colleagues to know. When they win, they want visible rewards—trophies, certificates, and Lucite pyramids that sit on the desk. Many Boomers' offices have a "wall of fame" displaying these tangible proofs of success. Rarely will you find such displays in the offices of workers from any other generation.

### The Counterculture in Command

When Boomers began to enter the workforce, uniqueness, individuality, or anything that made a person stand out from the crowd was not encouraged by the Matures. They believed the best employee was a seamless, uniform member of a team whose individual needs should be suppressed for the good of the larger group. The workplace the Matures developed was heavily influenced by the military—not unreasonable since so many Matures had served in World War II or Korea. Military hierarchy still resonated in all aspects of the job, from the clothes employees wore to strict divisions within the ranks, from new hires to senior-level managers.

Boomers were far less imbued with the military culture of stratification and discipline, and they brought some of the 1960s' laid-back attitude with them to the workplace. Even before Boomers began assuming positions of leadership, the workplace had started to evolve and become more flexible—not just in the recognition of personal preferences and individual styles, but in deeper and more democratic ways that are still in place today.

First, the workplace became much more ethnically diverse. The military became fully integrated when President Harry S. Truman issued an executive order on July 26, 1948, but the rest of society didn't follow suit immediately. The Equal Rights Amendment was passed by Congress 24 years later in 1972 and sent to the states for ratification. If enough states had ratified it, this would have meant that in the workplace white males would no longer be the only people with opportunities to climb the corporate ladder. Minorities and women, who had previously been relegated to jobs as servants, factory workers or other physical labor, and entry-level positions within organizations, would now be offered the opportunity to excel in a variety of jobs if they chose to do so. Granted, change has come slowly. With the stroke of a pen laws can be changed, but changing the minds of employers takes much longer, and many would argue that full integration has still not been achieved in today's workplace. But there are nevertheless far more opportunities than existed a few decades ago.

Second, the workplace became more democratic. Decisions were no longer made by one or two people in charge. It was no longer "my way or the highway." Instead, committees and focus groups met to discuss policies and procedures, large and small.

Still, even today, it's the top executives who get to say the final word for most businesses. They are deferred to, respected, and obeyed, but now it is Boomers instead of Matures who make those decisions and run their companies. Even though some dress codes have changed and group projects are the rule of the day, there is still a boss who climbed the ladder running most companies.

## Newer and Fewer Jobs

In the 1970s and 1980s, during the Boomers' ascendancy to top management, the United States began to move from a manufacturing-based economy to a service- and technology/information-based economy.

No longer was it necessary for the entire team to be at work at the same time to accomplish a desired goal. Employees could now, in theory, work in separate places and at staggered hours (not at home,

*Most Abundant Jobs in 1970 (in millions)*

| 1. | Equipment operators | 14,335 |
|---|---|---|
| 2. | Clerical workers | 14,208 |
| 3. | Professional and technical workers | 11,561 |
| 4. | Crafts workers | 11,052 |
| 5. | Laborers | 8,751 |

*Most Abundant Jobs in 1995 (in millions)*

| 1. | Technical administration and support | 13,841 |
|---|---|---|
| 2. | Professional specialists | 13,300 |
| 3. | Executives, administration, and management | 12,975 |
| 4. | Technical sales | 8,362 |
| 5. | Equipment operators | 7,136 |

however) but still contribute what was needed to achieve the final result. The individuals who comprised the teams no longer needed to stand shoulder to shoulder to create the product; they could now work from separate places and still get the job done.

The opportunities created by the North American Free Trade Agreement (NAFTA) began to threaten what manufacturing still remained in the United States. Manufacturing facilities began to leave this country to take advantage of a cheaper labor force in Mexico. Now, not only had the nature of Boomers' work changed, they were being replaced by much less expensive labor. And this trend continued into the 1990s, when manufacturing began to move to Asia in a successful search for even cheaper labor.

The bottom line is that the kinds of businesses Boomers now manage, what they produce, and the work their employees actually

> In 1989, the Boomers' pretax income was half as much as their parents' income was in 1960, when adjusted for inflation.

do have changed dramatically since they first entered the job market. The irony is that Boomers were both lifted by the rising economy and burned by it. They began to question the work ethics and behaviors they had been trained to think they needed in order to achieve success. "What did all that really do for me?" they asked. "I did what I was told to do, the way I was told to do it, and now I'm out of work. This isn't the way it was supposed to work out. What happened?"

Today the workplace continues to evolve. Even the technology-based economy we thought was recession-proof and a guarantee of good jobs is changing. Corporations and agencies in local, state, and national government are shipping technology assignments abroad to benefit from the cheap labor. Customer service call centers have moved from the United States and are now operated in India, even though you dial a local number from your home phone to ask a question about your local power bill.

## The Yoke of Loyalty

Baby Boomers began their careers with the same blind trust in their employers that their parents had felt. Matures, who had one, maybe two, jobs in a lifetime, participated in a compact, the unspoken commitment of loyalty between the employees and employer. One side's loyalty and trust generated an equal loyalty and trust on the other side.

Such employees often retired after long careers with a single company, many staying in the same department for their entire working lives. They moved up in a company as if they were riding a moderately fast elevator that went straight up. For example, an employee might start as a line worker, move to the position of line team leader, then to line supervisor, and finally to shift supervisor, overseeing the product output on that line.

That was the way things happened before the mid-1970s or early 1980s. Boomers entered the workforce with this as their model. They had become a significant portion of the workforce by the time lifetime employment came to an end.

The workplace has become uncomfortable for Boomers. On-the-job habits they learned aren't proving as valuable as they think they should be. They see employees their children's age operating with a different workplace value system, a value system that, when they were young, would have gotten them fired. Yet these kids are succeeding, and they seem to be playing by a new set of rules that the Boomers not only don't understand, but have never seen before.

## Downsized!

The effects of corporate downsizing may have been exaggerated, but many middle managers have been hurt. If they wish to reenter the market, they generally have to accept lower pay. The average worker reentering the job market between 1990 and 1992 took a pay cut of around 20 percent.

Boomers were hit particularly hard. They were often the most recent hires and got caught in the last-in, first-out eliminations. Or they had moved into lower management levels, which, when cut, saved the company the most money with the fewest layoffs. Boomers' model of the workplace had just been turned on its ear. Everyone knew someone who was hit by downsizing, if they weren't themselves. Workers were caught unaware and unprepared. Their loy-

### Big Blue Blues

 In the 1970s and 1980s, economic adjustment caused some of the nation's oldest, most recognizable, and most stable companies to lay off employees. Called *repositionings*, *rightsizings*, and *downsizings*, the simple, straightforward term is *layoffs*. I remember as a child riding with my mother through the streets of our hometown and passing an IBM facility. I'll never forget her saying, "If you get a job with IBM, you'll never have to look for another job again. They are a good company to work for."

The IBM layoffs hit the country in the gut because you knew things were seriously wrong when IBM had to cut the workforce. Although the company hated to use the word *layoff* and preferred *management-initiated separations*, in 1991 10,000 IBM employees "separated" from the company. By 1993, the total number of separations amounted to an estimated 25,000.

alty and commitment to the company and the years of hard work (read long hours) went unrewarded.

Many Baby Boomer managers and even the remaining Matures admit to very mixed feelings: They have to deal with both the bottom line and the human element in this new Boomer/Gen X/New Millennial mix. And that is the real conundrum we face. On one hand, creative, new blood in the workplace is very important (not to say inevitable), propelling a company's technology into the stratosphere along with profits. On the other hand, Boomers who have worked long hours every day can become very frustrated with the new work ethics, attitudes, and value systems that younger generations bring with them to the workplace, and this does have an impact on effectiveness and profits.

Does this mean most of the problems in the workplace are all about age? Not completely. The Boomers thought they had the same safety net as the Matures.

So what did Boomers do? Did they invent new strategies to deal with this new world order that had descended upon them? Most of them did not. They found other jobs, they began working long and hard, and they became loyal to their employers—all over again. This was shortsighted behavior, because the turbulent economic times that began in the 1980s weren't a temporary lapse. Layoffs have continued; they ebb and flow with the economy. We've seen incredible economic highs since the 1980s, and we've seen economic doldrums, too. And with each low comes more turnover.

A Boomer friend in Dallas, who works for a multinational technology company, told me that many of her peers in the office are still loyal to their company, but they realize that they could be laid off at any moment.

---

A Baby Boomer spoke to me about her father:

"My father would have a hard time in today's workplace. He'd encounter young employees who feel entitled to vacation days, sick leave, bonuses, and promotions—rather than earning them the hard way, as he did. He'd encounter a generation of employees who view the customers as obstacles to their day, not their reason for being at work. He'd encounter employees who view their job as an intrusion on their lives. I'm afraid he'd be flummoxed. He'd find his attitude of hard work, commitment to the customers, and perseverance a rarity in today's employees.

"And he'd say, 'What's wrong with today's kids?'"

"They're angry and afraid," she said. "There is so much uncertainty. We were a group that entered the workforce and thought our paths were set, and we're finding out that they're not. And do you know what? Most of us still won't change the way we operate. A few of my friends are becoming more entrepreneurial and making decisions based on their own personal satisfaction, but most of us are here plugging away for the company, knowing that the company has no loyalty at all for us. We don't like our jobs, but we can't stop working hard; we don't know how."

Despite the uncertainty, Baby Boomers are still hardwired for work. They make huge sacrifices in order to succeed. It's not surprising that many of them don't like their jobs or their work hours, and they hope their children won't have to experience the same anxieties. But they keep on keeping on. They're awarded new titles, promotions, a window office, and another engraved Lucite paperweight for their desk, which everyone coming into their office will see. They understand that their employers have no loyalty to them at all, yet they're still company men and women.

They're succeeding; they're winning. And more and more of them are coming to me and telling me in private that they wish they could change their behavior, but, like my friend in Dallas, they don't know how.

## Generational Voices

*Subject:* **Cici Thompson, CAE**
*Age:* **55**
*Location:* **Washington, D.C.**
*Title:* **Vice President, Meetings and Membership**
*Employer:* **Employee Relocation Council (ERC)**

*Cam Marston: Describe your generation's attitude today.*

*Cici Thompson:* Enjoying life, concerned about retirement, concerned about the state of the world. Hoping my kids do well.

*C.M.: What about your attitude toward work?*

*C.T.:* I'm at the office 12 hours a day. And I usually take work home.

*C.M.: Do you see different age groups in your office making time commitments similar to yours?*

*C.T.:* I see a real divide between my age group and the young people. There is a big difference between those in their early to midtwenties. In fact, I had someone just tell me she was going to resign, because she watched me and said she's not going to have that kind of life.

*C.M.: How did that make you feel?*

*C.T.:* [*Laughing*] Thoroughly depressed!

*C.M.: Who is going to take over for you and your generation when you're gone?*

*C.T.:* I don't know; probably a lot more people. One of the things I've found is that my generation does not know how to say "no." We keep taking more things on. One of the things I see with the younger generations is that when I tell them I want them to do something they'll say, "Fine, but my plate is full. So what do you want me to give up?"

*C.M.: What incentives work with your generation?*

*C.T.:* A combination of status/position that leads to monetary rewards, and the other is physical comfort.

*C.M.: Do those incentives apply to other age groups?*

*C.T.:* To some extent, yes. I see that working for positions is very important, and money is an important issue, but they're not willing to sacrifice their free time for either of these.

*C.M.: Do you ever change the way you speak or the language you use when dealing with the members of different generations?*

C.T.: Yes. I'll be more respectful of those who are older than I am. I'll be more direct with people my own age, and I tend to use more jargon when I'm around my children's friends—younger conversation. The same is true at work.

C.M.: *Do you see the younger employees changing their language for you?*

C.T.: I haven't noticed that.

C.M.: *How do you celebrate success at work?*

C.T.: A glass of wine. The same with failure. When something goes over very well with one of our events we usually take everyone out to a really nice lunch.

C.M.: *When someone younger than you comes to your office for your help, do you expect them to behave in a way that plays to your seniority or your title?*

C.T.: I guess I have to say yes, I do, but I'm trying to overcome that.

C.M.: *Why?*

C.T.: I think it is putting too much emphasis on me to think that someone should change the way they talk to me.

C.M.: *Is it important to you that you fit in your office place?*

C.T.: Yes.

C.M.: *How do you define fit?*

C.T.: I want everyone to like me.

C.M.: *When someone new comes into the workplace, how do you know whether they'll fit? What do you look for?*

C.T.: Somebody who is forthright and has a good sense of humor. If I get the impression that I'm interviewing Eddie Haskell, that turns me off right away. I look for a sense of honesty and that they're going to take a job and run with it.

*C.M.: How much of your work ethic of 12 hours per day and taking work home are you looking for out of new hires? Is it important to you?*

*C.T.:* No. I want the ability to do it, but I'd encourage them not to do it.

*C.M.: What is your generation paranoid about?*

*C.T.:* My biggest fear is that before I'm ready to leave, I'm cast out. I've heard horror stories about people who are fired just before their retirement kicks in, and I don't want that to happen.

*C.M.: Are you doing anything to make sure that doesn't happen?*

*C.T.:* I'm trying to broaden my understanding of the organization and trying to contribute as much as I can.

*C.M.: Define success.*

*C.T.:* Feeling that you have accomplished something, and people are looking at what you accomplished and are saying, "That was really good."

*C.M.: Hypothetical example: A young person is coming into the workplace, and you have the opportunity to sit them down and say, "This is what you need to know to be successful here." What would you tell them?*

*C.T.:* How important it is to work independently and to seek advice when necessary and to know when seeking advice is necessary. And to work as part of a team and to know how important the whole team is.

*C.M.: How important are work relationships with others?*

*C.T.:* The few people that I've not gotten along with in the past have made it very difficult to work together.

*C.M.: When you remember the good times, what are they?*

*C.T.:* Celebrating successes. As a group, when we've done something great we sit back and say, "Aren't we terrific!"

*Subject:* **Anonymous**
*Age:* **Boomer/Xer**
*Location:* **Midwest**
*Title:* **Manager**
*Employer:* **Bank**

*Cam Marston: What incentives work for your generation? What about you personally? What makes you want to work harder?*

*Anonymous:* Well, just so you know, I think I fall at the tail end of the Boomers and the beginning of the Xers. I was born in 1960. For me personally, title is very important. Recognition is probably the second, and compensation is probably the third.

*C.M.: When you say "recognition," what does that mean?*

*Anon.:* If I've worked really hard on something, I want the recognition for doing that work—probably from my boss and probably from peers. That recognition is very important to me. It's a strong motivator. I want work to be recognized.

*C.M.: In what form do you want the recognition? Do you want the boss to come to you personally, to make an announcement, to put you in the newsletter, or all of the above?*

*Anon.:* It can be really good for the boss to just give you that feedback, "You did a good job!" But you also don't want it to happen where you did all the work, the boss says you did a good job, but it's not known by others that you did that work. That's a really bad feeling for my generation. So, I would say publicly, yes, you want the feedback from the boss that you're on track and doing well. But I also think if it's a large-scale initiative or a big project, you want that recognition to go beyond your immediate supervisor.

*C.M.: Let's say you've had a great promotion or your team has done something remarkable. How do you celebrate success?*

*Anon.:* We've worked really hard here on culture. We have brief meetings weekly to talk about weekly successes or weekly concerns, so you're celebrating with your peers frequently. You talk about what you feel good about and what worked successfully and what your numbers were for the week. So it's kind of a neat way to celebrate. We have achievement awards, newsletters, all kinds of things like that.

*C.M.: Is the weekly meeting important? Could it be biweekly or monthly? Or do you feel weekly is the best way?*

*Anon.:* Weekly seems to be really good to reinforce the culture.

*C.M.: Tell me more about your frequent meetings. Are they regularly scheduled?*

*Anon.:* They are set at the same time every week. It is a time for us to celebrate one another's success and pass the word when someone else has done well.

*C.M.: Is there one generation that responds to this more than another? Or is it across the board?*

*Anon.:* It seems to work across the board. It's that act of coming together, but it probably resonates more with the Boomers.

*C.M.: What are the most glaring incorrect stereotypes about your generation? Knowing that you were born in 1960, you're kind of a member of two generations. So, set a foot in each generation. What do you think are the incorrect stereotypes of the Boomers and Generation X?*

*Anon.:* The one I think is correct for the Boomers is: "Hard work will always help you move up the ladder."

*C.M.: Is it accurate?*

*Anon.:* Maybe that falls under incorrect because I think there is the stereotype that if you work hard, you'll move up, you'll do well, and that's not always the case. There's politics involved, so that might actually fall in the category of not necessarily being true. But, there's a real perception that you have to work hard to move. It is the belief in the strong work ethic and the desire to give 110 percent. It probably tends to create a stressed group, because you're trying to be very motivated in all of those areas. And there are a few more stereotypes about the Boomers.

*C.M.: Such as?*

*Anon.:* I think we have a very clear sense of the difference between right and wrong. For Boomers, things tend to be black or white. Either it's right or it's wrong. I think as Xers, the distinction is maybe not as clear.

*C.M.: Xers see things much more as gray?*

*Anon.:* Yes. They're able to rationalize things a little bit more.

*C.M.: What does fit mean? Is it important to you that you're a "fit" at your office? What happens to those who don't fit?*

*Anon:* That's probably a little bit different for me as a human resources person because the HR people don't necessarily fit; we're typically on the outside anyway. But I think, in general, people want to blend in; to be accepted. But, as an HR person, what we strive for is an inclusive work environment. We want a mix of people who bring diversity, not only of race and gender, either, but of thinking styles and experiences. So, as HR people, we strive for mixture, we strive to create something where there isn't necessarily a fit, but that's why I said HR is probably a little different.

*C.M.: What, if anything, is your generation paranoid about?*

*Anon.:* I think we are probably paranoid about job loss, lack of employer loyalty, and the continuous threat of economic downturn.

*C.M.: Does it go across generational boundaries, or is there any part of that paranoia that is unique to your age group?*

*Anon.:* I don't know that the Xers have that fear. I think the Xers think, "Okay, if I can't be here, I'll end up somewhere else." I think maybe the Boomers and the Matures have it.

*C.M:   How do you think your generation will be remembered?*

Anon.: I think we will be remembered for the advancements in space and technology and medical advances. That's how I think we will be tagged. Huge leaps in medicine, for sure.

*C.M.: What steps are necessary to become successful, and how do you get there?*

*Anon.:* For me personally, success is the balance between work and family. And I am coming to understand that I won't be remembered for my successes here at work, but I will be remembered for my successes with my family. I think we have a commitment to make a difference. That's a part of me. I have a commitment to make a difference in not only the lives that are immediately around me but others as well. And how do you get there? I think the successes are often little ones. I think you have to be aware of the feedback, but sometimes we're too busy to see it. I think the successes are on a daily basis.

*C.M.: What about heroes?*

*Anon.:* Heroes for my generation are definitely the early astronauts: Alan Shepherd, John Glenn, Gus Grissom, Gordon Cooper, Neil Armstrong. Those guys are really big heroes for my generation because they went somewhere and did something that was viewed as impossible. You know, they accomplished something very quickly. Billy Graham is someone who has really touched my generation. JFK was one on my list. Norman Schwarzkopf—he is someone who really touched my generation.

And then you had defining moments. I think landing on the moon, the assassinations of JFK and Bobby Kennedy, the *Challenger* explosion, Watergate, and Richard Nixon's resignation. I have Desert Storm—that may fall under Xers, though. And the suppression of the student uprising in Tiananmen Square in China is one of those that I have a real visual on. Those people lay down in front of tanks. That's an image that will always stick with me. And the fall of Communism.

*C.M.: What about motivators for the generations?*

*Anon.:* The Xers that I have working for me are motivated more by time off, wanting quality family time and life balance. That's very important and, since I'm kind of borderline, I have a real need for that, too. But I also know I'm a workaholic, and I have this strong work ethic and this desire to move up the ladder. So, I'm kind of a blended animal, but I do think Xers are motivated by time off, life balance, and flexibility.

*C.M.: Have you had any of your Xers, or even any Boomers, turn down opportunities because they didn't want the responsibilities the promotion entailed?*

*Anon.:* Yes, we have. They are probably around 30 years old. Most of the time it's young families who say, "No, I don't want that promotion. I don't want that additional responsibility while I have young children." Often, "while I have young children" is tagged onto that. People who don't have children don't understand that.

# 4 | Gen X—How They Got Here

## Cynical? Questioning? Cautious? You'd Better Believe It

Gen Xers were born between 1965 and 1979. Some of them were the children of Matures, but most were the offspring of the senior members of the Baby Boomer generation. Like all parents since the world itself was born, Xers' parents wanted more for their kids than they'd had, and they were ready to make the sacrifices they thought were necessary to provide it.

### How They Grew Up

For Boomers, it was important for their children to be well educated and upwardly mobile. In many households that meant both parents working—long and hard, in true Boomer style. They came home tired at the end of every long day, often worn out and emotionally ragged from the stress of office politics.

Their youngest kids were put in day care and then in preschool, to be picked up midafternoon by babysitters or nannies. Many school-age children were left home alone after class, with strict rules not to answer the door if a stranger came by and to be nice to their siblings. As soon as their parents got home, they started preparing dinner and reviewing the children's homework while they all caught up on each other's day. Children often heard their parents complain about how hard they worked and how tired they were. And always, parents felt guilty about leaving the kids at home alone or with only a sitter during the day.

When they weren't home alone, Gen Xers and New Millennials were among the most programmed children of all time. The idea of play had shifted from simple after-school activities and sports to enrichment programs and professional coaching, a natural offshoot of their Boomer parents' competitive approach toward work. An entire new segment of the auto industry—the minivan—was developed to meet the needs of the Boomer soccer moms and dads.

This does not even begin to address the disruptive effects that divorce and remarriage(s) or single parenthood had on Gen Xers and New Millennials, to say nothing of the challenges these young people faced forging new relationships with step-siblings and half-siblings and creating new family circles when possible. Between the late 1960s and mid-1970s, the divorce rate in the United States doubled.

At the center of all these very complex currents and crosscurrents, Gen Xers became adults in a culture wholly different from the one in which Boomers had come of age.

**Stiff Competition**

From early childhood through their college years, Gen Xers heard their parents talking about their hopes for them:

I hope you . . .

- Do well in school.
- Go to college.
- Get a master's degree.

- Become a professional.
- Be your own boss.

. . . so you don't have to . . .

- Work as hard as I do.
- Pinch pennies like I do.
- Work for a jerk like I do.

What did these poignant desires mean for Gen Xers as they began entering the workplace in the late 1980s and early 1990s at a time when the economy was floundering? Not a lot. Xers were often competing for jobs with their Gen X peers and laid-off and downsized Baby Boomers. Financial publications predicted Gen X would be the first generation in the nation's history to be less successful than their parents.

As *Time* magazine reported in "Great Xpectations," June 9, 1997:

"Boomers," born from 1946 to 1964, grew up in affluence: economic progress was assumed, freeing them to focus on idealism and personal growth. Young Xers, however, lurched through the recession of the early '80s, only to see the mid-decade glitz dissipate in the 1987 stock-market crash and the recession of 1990–91. Gen X could never presume success. In their new book *Rocking the Ages*, Yankelovich's Walker Smith and his colleague Ann Clurman blame Xers' woes on their parents: "Forget what the idealistic boomers intended," Xers say, "and look at instead what they actually did: Divorce. Latchkey kids. Homelessness. Soaring national debt. Bankrupt Social Security. Holes in the ozone layer. Crack. Downsizing and layoffs. Urban deterioration. Gangs. Junk bonds . . ."

It was a buyers' market—employers could choose to hire either a young, unproven Gen X worker or an experienced Boomer employee who already knew how the workplace functioned and was eager to reclaim an income to pay the bills and debts incurred by adulthood. Boomers obviously had the edge. No wonder so many Gen Xers have a slight feeling of pessimism.

**Hours versus Output: Where the Disconnect Begins**

A major difference between Boomers and Gen Xers is their work habits, and for many on both sides it has become a bone of contention. Boomers think getting the job done means putting in long, visible hours. They have a stereotypical idea of Gen X employees as slackers who are unwilling to put in enough time. But Gen Xers think of hard work as *effective output*, and they are unwilling to put in long hours if they have produced the output necessary for that day.

A Gen Xer might say, "Yes, I work hard. I bust my hump to get everything done so that I can go home on time." This disturbs and confuses the Boomers, who, especially when they were young, got to the office early—earlier than the boss—and avoided leaving before the boss did because they wanted literally to be seen as hard workers. Gen Xers are less concerned about who sees them at the office. In short, Boomers' definition of hard work has largely been rejected by the younger generation.

One reason for this is that Gen Xers and Millennials grew up observing their parents' roller-coaster ride in the workplace: layoffs, downsizings, so-called management-initiated separations, difficulties with their bosses and other employees, and years of hard work that has not rewarded them for their efforts as they expected. This is where the first real disconnect between the generations in the workplace today begins.

**Plus . . .**

There are other reasons Gen Xers see work differently than Boomers do:

■ Sheer numbers tell the tale: Gen X is vastly outnumbered by Boomers, who total 77 million to the Xers' 44 million. There are too few Xers to compete with the enormous generation of Boomers that precedes them.

- The top echelons of the workplace are already filled with Baby Boomer managers who have no intention of moving aside or leaving.
- The on-deck circles—or the paths for promotion—for management positions are also crowded with the millions of Boomers who came before the Xers and who work feverishly to claim those promotions for themselves.
- Gen Xers seem to have little incentive to push hard, since pushing hard yields no immediate results. Remember that this is the generation raised on the theories behind *Sesame Street*—quick learning and quick results.
- Gen Xers' competitive skills are clearly not as well honed as those of Boomers, who spent decades following the workplace rules of competition and rules of engagement for success. Nor do Boomers necessarily share their knowledge of the rules with their Gen X peers.

### Gen X = Prince Charles?

 A good way to understand the Generation X career outlook is to compare Gen Xers to England's Prince Charles. He has a pretty good job, has some accomplishments to his name, and is a noted figure. But he's limited as to how far he can go until his mother, Queen Elizabeth, steps aside. And there are no signs of her doing that any time soon. She's healthy and active and keeps a full agenda. Likewise, Generation Xers have experienced some success in their careers thus far but they are limited in how far they can go with the healthy, active, and busy Boomers blocking their paths.

## A Question of Values

Gen X also questions a number of Boomer value systems, starting with the concepts of what constitutes a successful career and the validity of the Boomer work ethic. If asked, "What does it take to be successful here?" a Boomer might answer, "To do well here, or anywhere, you need a strong work ethic, you need to become a member of the team, and you need to be loyal. Be patient. Understand you'll have to make sacrifices for this company," and similar exhortations.

Gen X has seen something else: "Hey, our Boomer parents and their friends embraced these workplace values and got burned, downsized, laid off, and bankrupt."

Gen Xers' idea of success is different, and for good reason. Many of them grew up in Boomer households with both parents working, and they have seen the results of a strong work ethic—the long hours away from home, the stress induced by workplace competition—and say, "Why bother? Do I really need to do this? Is what I do at this job truly valuable? Or are these values more likely to make me vulnerable to the inevitable workplace changes?"

This is where the Gen Xers and to some extent the New Millennials have parted ways with their Boomer bosses (and parents). The result is a 180-degree difference in the way they define success in the workplace.

Their definition is simple: Money is good, but control of your time is the primary goal.

## Feet of Clay

When Gen Xers entered the workplace, they brought with them a new and slightly cynical perspective. It's rare to find a Gen Xer who isn't dissatisfied with something, although it's hard to pinpoint exactly what the dissatisfaction is about. They don't like the idea of being victims, but if you consider the world they grew up in, you can see how at the very least a certain pessimism might develop.

For instance:

- They (and the rest of us for that matter) have been failed in one way or another by every pillar of society, whether government, the military, big business, or even the Catholic Church, which for years vigorously denied any type of wrongdoing.
- Watergate unfolded on television in front of a nation voracious for the bad news. From that time on, elected officials were much more likely to be regarded with distrust.
- Layoffs occurred throughout the nation, and the companies doing the firing were those that, only a few years earlier, had made unspoken but still very real commitments to their lifelong employees. Many of the corporate casualties were Gen Xers' parents.
- The war in Vietnam cast a pall on the military and the civilians running it. What were they really doing over there? Was this our fight to begin with? The Boomers were asking tough questions and Generation X watched the television as the nation's leaders were unable to give solid, responsible answers.
- Even the press, which was held in such high regard by the Boomers for exposing Watergate and for publishing the Pentagon Papers, began to lose much credibility for the Xer generation as media outlets increasingly fell under the sway of corporate owners and sensationalist profit motives.

How valid is this view? Does Gen X really have a reason to be as pessimistic as they seem to be? From my surveys and conversations with Gen Xers, the answer is: "Probably."

When the boss says, "This is so," do Gen Xers have a good motive to question whether it is right, or whether the boss is shading the truth or outright lying? Probably.

Gen Xers are more likely than earlier generations to *dis*believe what their leaders say, or just as likely to silently think, "What is the true motive here? What is in it for him/her/them?" Such suspicion of people in power is unfortunate, but it is also pervasive among Xers. They've learned in their lifetimes that what people say and what they do are often drastically different.

## Carpe Diem in the Workplace

How has this translated to the workplace? After all, Gen Xers do recognize that they have to pay the rent and feed, clothe, and educate their families—just like everyone who came before them.

Given the current economic environment, Gen X has opted for a different approach: carpe diem in the workplace. When I interview them, this is typical of what they tell me:

> Since there is no guaranteed future, I will take from this job whatever I can get. The values that the Boomer bosses tell me I need to adopt are betraying them right and left as they're axed from their jobs.

> Why in the world would I adopt their attitude? The only thing I know for sure that will happen is today, and I'm going to enjoy today—and tomorrow and the next day. I understand that the future is inevitable, but I'm not going to base my daily work behavior on an outcome that I can't control, a promise controlled by someone else who's probably untrustworthy, so I'll make sure today is a quality day.

This does not mean Gen Xers don't plan for the future; they do. They invest in the 401(k) plans, the Roth plans, and the like, but they aren't willing to become workaholics for the benefit of the company—it's too risky.

## Everybody Needs a Hero

Gen X also has a very different attitude toward role models and heroes than Boomers and Matures have. The contrast is quite striking. Most Xers are reluctant to put faith in anyone they don't actually know. Because leaders in every branch of society have failed them, Gen X believes that these leaders will continue to fail when their true motives are exposed, as they almost inevitably will be.

In fact, you'd have a hard time finding a single person that this generation admires wholeheartedly. According to J. Walker Smith and Ann S. Clurman in *Rocking the Ages*:

> The Matures' heroes are groups or teams of people. They're likely to cite the Army or Marines as their heroes. Ask them to be specific and they'll cite the men of the Normandy invasion or the Marines of the Pacific Island wars, but seldom will they mention an individual as a hero.
>
> The Boomer heroes were people with a charismatic message and great visions of opportunity and equality for all. The Kennedy family is often listed, as is Dr. Martin Luther King, Jr. These leaders said, "Follow me to a better place," and the Boomers largely followed. In fact, the Boomers still follow those same leaders today. Their heroes remain individuals who represented the hopes and desires of a large group of people. They were charismatic people whose beliefs galvanized their entire generation.

This doesn't mean there are no heroes for Gen X. That is not true at all. Some of the most fascinating and startling things I have learned studying the different generations are:

First, Generation X has no shared heroes—no Martin Luther King, John Kennedy, Dwight Eisenhower, or Charles Lindbergh. Generation X has seen the notable individuals of their time repeatedly knocked from their pedestals, either through something they've done or through the deep penetration of the media into their lives. They've become skeptical about anyone who steps out in front of the crowd and says, "This is who I am. Follow me." Repeatedly those people have been caught lying, and there is a great risk in following them—the greatest risk being disillusionment.

Second, Generation X has chosen heroes from among the people they know personally—family members, educators, coaches, employers, and others with whom they have immediate and ongoing contact. These are people that Gen Xers can reach out to and touch. They can shake hands with the boss or hug their fathers. Like Matures and Boomers, they need heroes, but they select people who have proven themselves to Generation Xers personally, who have passed the individual Xer's test, which simply is: "Do you do what you say and say what you do? Are you well-intentioned, and are you reliable?"

Many Gen Xers were latchkey kids who grew up home alone while both parents worked to pay the bills. As a result, the Xers have said to themselves: "I didn't get a lot of attention, mentoring, and leadership from my parents when I was a child, because they both worked. But that doesn't mean I don't want it now. It just means I have to search for a role model elsewhere."

Gen Xer employees want to get to the office, do their jobs, and go home. So it's ironic that, given their ambivalence about the workplace, that's where they search for their heroes, because it's where they spend the most time.

## Loyalty in the Workplace

The role models Gen X is searching for—their local, tangible heroes—are advocates who champion the Xers' efforts for success. (See Chapter 7 to find out how to become such a person.)

The concept of loyalty is an issue here. Gen Xers, because of their unique preference for choosing heroes from among the people they know personally, are not loyal to the company they work for. Instead, they are loyal to their bosses. An Xer will say, "I work for John," not "I work for XYZ Company." You frequently see that when a much-admired boss or manager leaves the company, Gen X employees who worked directly with him or her invariably follow, or, when the boss leaves, productivity drops dramatically. Many times, employees lobby within their company to be transferred to a different department because they prefer the boss in that department to

### The Technology Exception

While most Xers are loyal to the boss, in some professions they are still loyal to the job. Technology is one arena where this is true. To stay at the cutting edge of a rapidly changing industry, employees in technology fields will often change jobs to keep up with the most current technology. It is their way of staying viable in a profession that is constantly evolving. Their personal regard for the boss is less important to them.

their new one. Gen X understands perfectly well that the company is valuable to them, but it's the boss who receives the loyalty.

For generations, employees who disliked their bosses typically stayed put out of loyalty to the company. Patience and sacrifice were sometimes necessary to maintain a job, and employees understood that disliking the boss was often just part of that job; there was no recourse. Gen X, with their carpe diem mentality, decided that enduring a poor manager isn't worth the effort, and they will search to find the right person with whom to work. They have an intrinsic need to identify with this role model or hero, and they will actively change jobs until that person is found.

### Human Resources to the Rescue: Hire the Right *Boss*

Human resources (HR) departments are unfortunate scapegoats; they have come under fire for not finding the right type of employee when filling a slot that calls for a Gen Xer. I've heard this frequently in companies that struggle with turnover. HR people must learn that a better approach to the problem is to look at the boss for whom the Xer is or will be working. Is this person the right type of boss?

Chances are the boss is not the type of person Gen X is looking for. He or she may be a leader whose actions and words contradict one another—an incitement to distrust among Xers.

HR people and management often tell me they see hardworking Gen X employees in other companies, but when they attempt to hire away these employees for their own company, the Gen Xers won't come over because they're loyal to their individual bosses. HR managers have to begin to look at it differently. Instead of wondering what the other company is doing to get and keep these good employees, they learn who these employees' manager is, and then try to hire him or her, not the employees. If the employees are as good as they appear to be, it means they are loyal to their manager and they'll follow him or her to the new job.

Now that the oldest of the Gen Xers are in their late thirties, their workplace attitudes and habits are showing some signs of change. Because they are parents and have fixed responsibilities, they're beginning to slow their job-hopping somewhat. A troubled economy that hasn't produced more jobs doesn't help their job-change options, either. The youngest members of Generation X, born in the mid- to late 1970s, still exhibit the classic Generation X behavior. However, if their older generational cohorts are indicators of what is to come, adulthood, and specifically parenthood, will slow their impatience a bit.

## Daddy Bosses

Parenting, not surprisingly, is an important issue to a generation that grew up with frequently absent parents and Big Bird as Big Babysitter. In 1980 one effect that many sociologists noted was that in two-income households with latchkey kids, Generation X's Boomer parents began raising friends, not children. The guilt of not being there when the kids were home alone made parents want to become their children's friends, instead of their parents.

The result: Generation Xers often don't have a true parenting figure in their lives who has taught them right from wrong, good from bad. This is even truer for the New Millennials

Employers often tell me they feel as if their employees want them to serve as surrogate parents on the job. Gen X employees bring personal issues to their bosses to get their feedback. The truth is, in many cases these employees are indeed looking for a parent figure on the job. Successful workplaces with Generation Xers who work hard and work well would probably agree.

## Enter Technology: Generation X's Great Workplace Equalizer

Technology entered Generation X's homes as a toy. Unlike their parents, who regarded technology as science and related it to school, Xers knew at once that it was not to be feared, but instead to be enjoyed and explored. Technology has always been a friend to Generation X. Not only did they think computer games, such as Atari, Commodore, Pong, and others, were fun, they were cool, too, because their parents couldn't play! Gen Xers nationwide used computer technology with such freedom and abandon that its use spread widely once personal computers became more affordable with the introduction of the Apple IIc and the Commodore.

In contrast, the Boomers' first experiences with technology came when the early single-action (e.g., word processing and creation of legal forms) computers entered the workplace. The systems were physically huge, taking up entire rooms and requiring special heating and cooling systems to keep them from breaking down. The procedures for operating the computers were complicated and demanded a long, steep learning curve. MS-DOS and its several complex programming iterations were the Boomers' first experiences with word processing or data management, and one wrong keystroke could paralyze the computer and potentially disable the entire system.

And while the promise of technology was that it would shorten the workweek by speeding up the work, the truth soon became evident—technology would *lengthen* the time at the job for two reasons. First, it was difficult to operate, and it took time to figure it out. Second, when it worked smoothly, more was demanded of employees by employers.

## Youth Leads the Way

Generation X entered the workplace unafraid of technology. They eagerly figured it out, adapted the systems, modified them, and used them to their advantage. Through technology they could actually finish their work faster and go home. The Boomers resented these abilities, but struggled to catch up to Generation X's proficiencies. They watched on the sidelines as technology advanced and became more and more critical to a company's basic operations, while Generation X became the focal point of it all.

The introduction of technology to business operations immediately changed the dues-paying process in this one arena, which benefited Generation X. For the first time in history the youngest generation of employees controlled a critical aspect of business. Traditionally, the younger employees had served in apprentice roles and gradually learned a trade or craft well enough to practice it on their own. In the world of technology, the youngest employees were the only ones who knew how to operate it.

Senior executives with years of experience, a series of postgraduate degrees, and an accumulation of wealth earned from business acumen were helpless seated in front of the computer screen. They were embarrassed to have to call on their young employees to teach them how to center a piece of text on a page as they typed a document. Or they realized that if their executive assistant (a new title for secretary) were to leave them, they'd have to admit to someone else that they were helpless in such a critical element of this new business environment. This fear was unknown to Generation X.

*But it remains a major threat to Boomers.*

## Do Gen Xers Think about the Future?

The *Christian Science Monitor* ("The Grunge Generation Grows Up," by Kim Campbell, July 21, 2004) presented one Xer's thoughts about the future this way:

> He plans for the future, particularly for retirement. Not long after he was elevated to the head of his family's company, he established a 401(k) program for the firm's employees, a majority of whom are Xers, too. "I sort of think of [Social Security] as a joke," he says. "I don't think it's going to be around when I'm old enough to need it."

The *Monitor* also points to studies that suggest his attitude is shared by others of his generation.

> Yankelovich has found that Xers have their eyes on retirement at an earlier age than Boomers did. And the recent Reach Advisors survey found that 29% of Gen Xers versus 22% of Boomers were saving for retirement with 401(k) or other defined contribution plans.
>
> This is a generation that does not necessarily expect to have the same kind of financial security as their parents do. And that's a big change.

The New Millennial generation follows Generation X. Their experiences are much different than those of Generation X, as we'll soon see. All in all, Gen X is an anomaly of a generation—small in population, small in birth years—but very consistent in their beliefs. They are the unintended by-product of a Boomer generation that sought to change the world, and that's a hard act to follow. Generation X will forever live in the Boomers' shadow. It won't be easy for them to compare their contributions to our society to those of Boomers and Matures, and even what Millennials will do. That's because Gen X contributions will be predominantly in terms of attitude and values—hard to see. They're lurkers: They operate in the background, not engaging society to the degree that Boomers and New Millennials do—but they're quietly making their own mark, motivated largely by dissatisfaction with the world they've inherited, as evidenced by the interviews that follow.

## Generational Voices

*Subject:* **Diane Stapley**
*Age:* **Gen X**
*Location:* **Austin, Texas**
*Title:* **Director of Platform Strategy for Server and**
 **Workstation Products**

*Cam Marston: What are the biggest stereotypes of your generation? Are any correct? Do you fit any of them?*

*Diane Stapley:* I'd say the biggest stereotypes are that we're lazy, materialistic, and me-centric. Perhaps the latter two fit many of my generation, but I'd say there are definitely hard workers, too, people who strive and succeed from "nothing" starts and who try to make a difference for others as well. I might fit the materialistic stereotype in that I feel I've worked very hard to get where I am and that I've earned my comfort level in life.

*C.M.: Define success. Where does money come into play in your definition?*

D.S.: Success is being better off than my parents were and achieving more in life—also, exceeding their expectations. It's doing what anyone/everyone said I couldn't do. It's having as much money as needed to make my lifestyle and dreams attainable—just beyond living comfortably, not outrageously filthy rich, but able to do what I like and attain comfort within reason. But it's also about respect—

gaining the respect of peers in my career realm, and attaining recognition for my achievements. It's also about being able to help others, especially the less fortunate and those whose life stories have started similarly to mine—for example, making sure that young girls have enough information and encouragement to also pursue military careers, studies in engineering, et cetera, that for me was something of a stretch or unusual.

*C.M.: Who are the heroes of your generation? Why?*

*D.S.:* In reverse order, they're either people who stood out from the pack, who weren't afraid to go against the accepted grain, or who otherwise made a difference in the world. The people who come to mind are Colin Powell; General Norman Schwarzkopf; Nelson Mandela; Princess Diana of Wales; Sarah Ferguson, Duchess of York; Mikhail Gorbachev; and Ferris Bueller!

*C.M.: What moments define your generation? Bands? Songs? TV shows?*

*D.S.:* I think my generation [teens during the 1980s, college during the 1990s] is largely defined by our experiences in the mid-1980s to mid-1990s, the coming-of-age period for us. Even though many bad things may have happened during that time, I think we were very well isolated by our parents and elders who perhaps wanted to give us an idyllic childhood after they survived World War II or the 1960s and 1970s. In my case, my parents were young, born 1949 and 1951, and my dad was a Vietnam veteran, FWIW [for what it's worth].

I think of the following as defining ideas or moments for my generation: perestroika, Black Monday, the fall of the Berlin Wall, the Gulf War, the end of apartheid, the meteoric rise of Silicon Valley. Ballad songs from 1980s rock bands like Def Leppard, Bon Jovi, Ozzy Osbourne, Billy Idol, Duran Duran, Guns N' Roses, Metallica, MC Hammer, U2, Motley Crue, and Madonna are all the theme songs of our lives, which were lived as much as possible like the movies of our time—*St. Elmo's Fire, Ferris Bueller's Day Off*, et cetera. We grew up on the morals of *Growing Pains, Miami Vice*, and anything on MTV. We learned technology from *Max Headroom*, adult life from *Cheers*, and racial sensitivity from *The Cosby Show*, and we knew Pee-wee Herman back when he was in the *Playhouse* and not arrested red-handed.

In college, we started watching *90210*, *Real World* (where we first realized that AIDS happens to anyone, with the death of Pedro Zamora), *Melrose Place*, and *Baywatch*. We still listened to Aerosmith, and also to Nirvana and the Stone Temple Pilots. We all know where we were when we heard Kurt Cobain died. We would crank up the radio if one of "our" songs came on: "We Are the World," "We Are the Champions," "Winds of Change."

*C.M.: What is your generation paranoid about?*

*D.S.:* Losing material comforts, and not being (or the *perception* of not being) as good as the Joneses or the guy in the office next to us. We're worried about being perceived as striving for less than the highest goals and of losing or being labeled a loser.

*C.M.: What is your generation's attitude? Where did it come from? Is it different today in any ways than it was in the past?*

*D.S.:* Our attitude is: "We're not gonna take it," like the song. Also, "Never surrender," again like the song (sense a theme here?). We got this from 1980s movies, where the protagonist was always portrayed as winning in the end, whether it was in war, business, love, guerrilla Wall Street investments, et cetera. We expect that if we give it our all, we'll get the best of everything. It's different, or changing, today in that we've had a real eye-opening as a result of getting into the real world after college (no longer cocooned by our parents or dorms/fraternities/sororities), and as a very recent result of terrorism, economic slumps, and misbehavior of political and spiritual leaders, which has resulted in a disappointment and increased mistrust of leaders. I'd say the biggest eye-opener, though, has been a result of global connectivity: In a very real and immediate sense, we can see the result of our actions and the actions of others. We can actually see that boycotting designers who use sweatshops may improve life for child laborers. We can see that our consumerism or activism has impact on things like world hunger and terrorist regimes.

*Subject:* **Anonymous**
*Age:* **Boomer/Xer**
*Location:* **Southeastern United States**
*Title:* **Senior Vice President, Sales**
*Employer:* **Large national bank chain**

*Cam Marston: Describe your "tweener" generation's attitude in your youth versus today.*

*Anonymous:* I think we were a lot more hopeful in our youth. I'm sure that is common in all generations. Watergate is my first memory, and it didn't take long for us to become disillusioned and apathetic. Political mistrust has been a part of my life from the beginning, and now when politicians do wrong I almost expect it. It isn't surprising anymore. I don't expect them to be held up to any kind of higher standard.

*C.M.: Has your attitude toward politicians transferred to any other types of leadership, or does it stay only in the political world?*

*Anon.:* I used to expect leaders to know what they were doing, but after the 1980s I don't think that is true. Corporate greed—everyone is out for themselves.

*C.M.: Would you be surprised if your CEO was found to be lining his own pockets?*

*Anon.:* I don't think so. I've tried to put him on a pedestal, and I've heard him speak. He's a really cool guy. At the same time he did some really ruthless things to bring about his success. But he does do a lot of charitable good. I probably justify it in my mind that it is okay that he has so much money because he does so much charitable work. And he's built a company that is good to its employees and the community. But I wouldn't be surprised.

*C.M.: Do you think your generation's attitude will change over time?*

*Anon.:* Maybe September 11 will have an effect.

*C.M.: How will September 11 change things?*

*Anon.:* It may not change the way we look at other people, but it may change ourselves and what we think is important. For example, our generation, at least for women, has really had to struggle with a career and a family, and for the first time I think men have had that struggle now. Maybe we'll make the decisions that put our family at least equal with our job.

*C.M.: Do you have any heroes?*

*Anon.:* I don't think so.

*C.M.: Who do you think your parents' heroes were?*

*Anon.:* Probably FDR [Franklin Delano Roosevelt].

*C.M.: What would it take for you to have heroes? What would you want them to be like?*

*Anon.:* I think back then the media hid everyone's warts. And I think now we see that everyone has a good side and a bad side. So I don't think I could ever have a hero. But what would it take? John McCain was the closest thing I had to a hero—spoke up, cut through all the crap, and really addressed what my generation was thinking, although no one does anything about it.

*C.M.: Is your generation the victim of stereotypes, and are any of them correct?*

*Anon.:* As a "tweener" I don't think anyone knows we exist. My brother and sister are Boomers, and there are some things that are similar. My best friend is six years younger than me and I'm not like her, either.

*C.M.: What do you expect from your generation?*

*Anon.:* We're a bridge between the two. I feel for the Boomers, who aren't very technologically savvy, and for the Gen Xers, who can't relate. The Boomers are so amazed by technology, but they can't understand that it's not that amazing; it's not that hard—that's just what the spreadsheet does. The Boomers can't understand why we should put a product online, whereas Gen X is saying, "Of course we should put it online. Why wouldn't we?" My generation is this bridge between the two extremes.

*C.M.: What do you expect from yourself?*

*Anon.:* I do want to be a community leader. My generation isn't as caught up in the trappings of the previous generations, the trappings of power. We want the end result, but we don't need to have the club memberships to do it. We see that as impractical.

*C.M.: What do you consider success?*

*Anon.:* Financial security—a nice house, a nice car, the ability to spend and to give to charities. I'll know I'm successful when I can pass on significant money to two key charities. And being a success in my job. And to be helpful to those I'm coaching in work.

*C.M.: Does your generation share that definition?*

*Anon.:* Maybe not so much. Maybe the charity part of it. I don't know. There are so few of us.

*C.M.: What are the steps to becoming successful?*

*Anon.:* Education, hard work, knowing what the market wants; it is definitely demand-driven. Knowing about other people—some psychology. We hate office politics, but we put up with it since we know it is unavoidable. The next generation hates office politics even more.

*C.M.: What do you like about other generations?*

*Anon.:* There's not a whole lot I like about my parents' generation. I think the whole sexist thing has taken me a lot of time to climb out of. There was a definite definition of male work and female work. It was impenetrable.

*C.M.: And Gen X?*

*Anon.:* Generation X? I respect their ability to cut to the chase. They don't get bogged down. When they see a problem, they solve it; they don't try to make it more difficult. Their understanding of technology is huge. They don't think about using the computer; they just do it. Their approach to problem solving is more streamlined. They get the answer a lot quicker.

*C.M.: Why is that?*

*Anon.:* If I had to guess, I'd say they grew up online and with video games. They were alone more as children. Maybe they didn't go out with groups much. The people I know don't like to go with groups much. They don't like meetings. They get to work, go to their desk, do their work, and go home. There are other things they want to do, whereas my generation is used to being around each other, getting consensus, and team building. Gen X says, "We don't need a team. Let's just do it."

*C.M.: What pop culture things characterize your generation?*

*Anon.: The Brady Bunch, Gilligan's Island,* Madonna, *The Carol Burnett Show, Mary Tyler Moore, Bob Newhart, Love Boat, Sesame Street, Romper Room, The Electric Company, Happy Days.* We quote those things to each other at cocktail parties. Like *Airplane* and *Austin Powers.*

*C.M.: Prioritize money in your generation.*

*Anon.:* I think it is important. It is number one since it allows us to do everything we want.

*C.M.: How is your generation different in the way you prioritize money?*

*Anon.:* I think Xers like the money, but they want time more. Those ahead of me probably want money—there's a status symbol there.

*C.M.: Do you respect the Boomers?*

*Anon.:* Yes, I guess. I don't know. I guess I don't. I definitely respect the Matures; they went through a lot of hardship. I respect Gen Y after September 11, and I can't imagine being a child and having that happen.

*C.M.: What about Gen X?*

*Anon.:* I think I fear them more than respect them. They have so much more knowledge than we do. They seem to know what they want and they go get it. They'll speak up and get the salary they want. I'm sure they don't respect us since we're remnants of the old "do as you're told" system, and I'm learning from them how to go get what I want.


*Subject:* **Dianna Rosemier**
*Age:* **28**
*Location:* **Washington, D.C.**
*Title:* **Event Planner**
*Employer:* **BRAVO! Events by Design**


*Cam Marston: True or false: Young people today—your generation—don't want to work, don't like to work, or don't know how to work. They put in their minimal time on the job and then leave to do whatever. Why aren't they dedicated and committed the way they should be?*

*Dianna Rosemier:* I do not agree with this statement, as I have yet to have a job (postcollege) at which I have not ended up working 60 hours per week on a regular basis. (During college I worked 20 to 30 hours per week.) My work ethic is strong, and so is that of my friends. I am sure some in my generation fit the bill these managers describe, but I am certainly not one of them.

*C.M.: Do you enjoy work?*

*D.R.:* I must admit that I do not enjoy working such long hours. I feel that there are two reasons I end up working the hours I do:

One, employers are running companies much leaner than they

did in the past, so everyone must now do the job of two or more people. They lay people off and don't replace them, but they want the same amount of work to get done, so it falls on whoever is left.

Two, my desire to do a good job. I never want it to be said that I did not do the best that I was capable of. I place a great deal of pressure on myself to meet my deadlines and perform well. It would really bother me for an employer to insinuate or state that I did not do a good job. I guess this falls under personal responsibility/pride in one's work.

*C.M.: Why, then, do so many Gen Xers move from job to job?*

*D.R.:* The unrealistic demands of employers combined with a strong work ethic and desire to do well lead to burnout, which explains why so many of us do not stay with a firm for more than a year to two years. We simply get frustrated and fizzle out. Employers don't realize that we are burned out until it's too late.

*C.M.: What about personal sacrifice?*

*D.R.:* We also get tired of sacrificing our personal lives for an employer that could lay us off at any minute without hesitation. There used to be something to company loyalty, but the way companies have been run in the past 10 to 15 years has taken that away. I have seen layoffs and corporate buyouts and I am not even 30. I have seen the corporate disregard for hard work and loyalty, which becomes very apparent the moment a company starts to get into financial difficulty. The first things to be cut are employee benefits and jobs. Then company executives sit back and wonder why morale is low and why "these kids today" don't want to stick around.

*C.M.: What do you expect from a boss?*

*D.R.:* Fairness above all else. I don't want game-players who have a hidden agenda. I want an honest, intelligent boss, someone with whom I always know where I stand, someone who lets me know when I make a mistake and helps me to correct it, but who also offers praise when I do well and makes me feel like my efforts and opinions matter.

I can't stand micromanagement. If I make a mistake, let me know and suggest a couple of methods for correction (and ask for my input, as well). If, however, I do a good job and keep you informed, please don't try to babysit me. It just frustrates me and causes resentment.

I have had two really great bosses since college (and a couple during college), but I did have one horrible manager at my first job out of college. She was horrible at prioritizing tasks and everything was an emergency. She interrupted me several times a day with tasks, so I had a hard time getting larger projects done. I felt like I would put out one fire and have to immediately jump to another, while I could see three more starting to smolder, knowing I couldn't stop to keep them from becoming full-fledged, five-alarm fires. It was horrible, and I felt like I had no control and that eventually people might start thinking I was doing a bad job despite my lack of control, so I left.

*C.M.: What do you expect from a company?*

*D.R.:* I want a company that truly values its employees. Many companies talk about how they value their employees and feel that the team is important, but their actions belie their statements. This is evidenced by their eagerness to cut the head count and benefits when times get tough. I understand trimming the fat or getting rid of deadweight, but I have seen real performers, who in some cases gave great portions of their lives to a company, getting laid off.

If you truly value your people, then you treat them fairly. Respect their right to have a life outside of work, and encourage them to further develop their skills through training, new opportunities, et cetera. Ask for and actually listen to their input. You don't always have to agree.

*C.M.: What do you expect from a profession?*

*D.R.:* Fulfillment!!! For me (and many in my generation) personal fulfillment is where it's at. We want what we do to mean something and to be a reflection of who we are as people. We want to find our passion and make that our profession. We see no point in toiling away

40 to 60 hours a week doing something we don't really like for a company whose mission means nothing to us.

Our individual passions vary, but if we have an employer who recognizes us as individuals and encourages us to search out and fulfill our dreams, we will be loyal. Even if it turns out that in order to pursue our passions we must leave, we will do everything we can to help that employer, such as giving extra notice and offering to help hire and train a new person. We will also stay in touch and continue to help that employer in any way we can in the future. It may sound corny, but it's true.

I don't want to spend my life working for something I don't care about. If I find that my current job is not helping me discover or develop my passion, then I will leave. Sometimes an employer has control over that, but other times the employer and I must be honest with each other and say to one another, "I respect who you are and what you want to do, but unfortunately, it doesn't fit within my plan." That's okay as long as both parties walk away feeling that they served each other well in the meantime.

*C.M.: When you go to work for someone somewhere, what are your minimal expectations?*

*D.R.:* To be respected and valued as a human being, not just as a means of lining the company pockets. Fair pay. I am all for merit-based pay. If I do a better job than someone else with the same title, then pay me more. If you can't give me money, find another way of rewarding vision and superior performance. I want fairness, which may or may not mean equality. Benefits. My generation considers basic health, dental, and vision benefits a right. We don't mind paying for a portion of them, but if I don't have them and I am not given what I need to affordably obtain them, then I won't work for you. It's that specific.

*C.M.: How about your life versus your job?*

*D.R.:* The right to have a life outside of work is important. I don't want to work 60-hour weeks on a regular basis. I don't mind doing it on a short-term basis. But don't assign me a grueling, long-term project or bury me with so much work that the only way I can get it done is to put in an extra 20 unpaid hours each week. At a minimum, offer comp time (and actually let me use it) or something else that recognizes the extra work.

*C.M.: Vacation?*

*D.R.:* This is a frustrating topic. Don't make us earn it before we can use it. If we leave before what we have used is earned, we have no problem with it being deducted from our checks. That is fair. Please recognize that I have a life and though I am not married I do have a family I like to visit. Don't keep me from seeing them, or I will leave. I am not asking for six weeks; I am just asking for the standard two to three weeks and the ability to take it. There is nothing more frustrating than knowing that although you have earned vacation time, you can't use it because the workload doesn't allow it.

*C.M.: What makes a boss or a company likable?*

*D.R.:* The company—respect for employees and true leadership and vision. A mission statement means nothing if the person who created it doesn't really believe it. Phoniness can be spotted a mile away.

The boss—someone with strong morals, someone who still believes in treating others as they would want to be treated. Someone I can trust to do not only what is best for the company, but who will also try to do what they can for me as well. That can be anything from offering promotions where appropriate (and opportunity exists) to helping me identify and work on a weakness or further develop a strength.

*C.M.: Is it important that you like your company/boss?*

*D.R.:* Yes. I don't want to work for a company or individual whom I cannot respect. I can work with people I don't like (assuming the problem is strictly personality and not an inability to pull one's weight or a propensity to gossip or try to undermine others), but I particularly prefer that my boss not fall into that category.

*C.M.: What if you don't respect the boss?*

*D.R.:* I suppose it depends on the nature of the problem and how long I think the boss will be around or how long I will be in that particular position. I can stick things out if it is to my benefit to do so and if I do not believe that the person will intentionally try to hurt me.

*C.M.: Do you have a five- or ten-year plan?*

*D.R.:* Not really. I have some vague ideas of the course I am trying to shape and hone as I go along and learn new things about myself and what I like to do. Once I am further along in that process and have a better idea as to where I want to go, I will set specific goals and chart a course for reaching them.

*Subject:* **Matt Jones**
*Age:* **31**
*Location:* **Washington, D.C.**
*Title:* **Vice President**
*Employer:* **Leading Authorities Speakers Bureau**

*Cam Marston: What is your generation's attitude toward work today?*

*Matt Jones:* Quiet self-confidence. I do what I want to do, and I work pretty hard. It is a day-by-day attitude; people are just kind of enjoying themselves.

*C.M.: What incentives work with your generation?*

*M.J.:* They work for something they believe in deeply, or they're working for money. I'm not working at Leading Authorities because of the opportunities to send speakers around the country. I'm working here because I want to make a little money. I work hard to prepare myself to do the next thing.

*C.M.: Do you have a time line for doing something else?*

*M.J.:* I have a time line for doing something different, not going someplace else. I do something until I feel like I've got it down, and then it's time to do something different. If it's not challenging, I'm ready to do something else.

C.M.: *How does that differ from previous generations?*

M.J.: My father-in-law has been an accountant for the same association for 30 years, and there's no way that I could do that. I've been at my company for six years, and that's rare in my generation. Just about every time I've wanted an opportunity to do something different it has come my way. I respect my father-in-law's decision, but it confuses me. Sometimes I think it's a little odd. I suspect he thinks I'm unfocused. I think that, like a lot of people in my generation, we don't have an end goal professionally. My attitude is that if I work real hard at what I'm doing, new opportunities will present themselves and we'll see what happens next.

C.M.: *Let's talk about how you like to be approached in a sales call.*

M.J.: I like the sales call to proceed this way: Get right to the point. I don't like long business lunches. I don't like the first 45 minutes of long meetings, which essentially are people saying, "I'm going to make you feel good and you should make me feel good." How well I know a vendor is important, but at the end of the day it still comes down to the numbers. I'm not personally connected to someone just because I know they're putting kids through college.

C.M.: *How do you celebrate success at work?*

M.J.: Very briefly. We don't dwell on the successes very much here.

C.M.: *Do you have heroes?*

M.J.: I don't think we're old enough yet to have any big heroes. I don't think people in my generation put that much stock in our pop culture heroes. I look to the Greatest Generation [the Matures]. You can find tons and tons of heroes there. I'd be surprised if people in my generation found any heroes in the Baby Boomers. I think our generation views that generation very skeptically.

*C.M.: What about incorrect stereotypes?*

*M.J.:* I think it's that we don't care, that there's a lackadaisical attitude I think most people work hard at whatever they make up their mind to do. They work hard and they play pretty hard. They try hard to enjoy themselves and to enjoy their lives. Right or wrong, our generation is viewed sometimes as rude.

*C.M.: Is it important that you're a fit in your office?*

*M.J.:* I don't think so.

*C.M.: What are the characteristics of someone you'd like to work with?*

*M.J.:* Honest. Creative. Funny. Un-PC. Refreshing.

*C.M.: How about someone you dislike?*

*M.J.:* Someone who has an ulterior motive, puts on airs, or is caught up in titles. They are there to call a lot of attention to themselves— they're self-centered.

*C.M.: What does a good work ethic mean to you?*

*M.J.:* Someone who takes their job seriously and works hard at it. Doing a good job at what you do. I think doing something right is more important than spending time at it. When you first mentioned work ethic, I didn't think of someone who spent a lot of time at the office working until late at night. People with a good work ethic see things through and make sure things are done right.

*C.M.: Do you think your generation has expectations for itself?*

*M.J.:* I would have said "no" except in this last year, I think that our generation has become one that is prepared to do something. I think if our generation had been called on to serve in the war, we would have done so and we would have done well.

*C.M.: Is your generation paranoid about anything?*

*M.J.:* Security. It's not uncommon to talk about money with your friends in more detail than is traditional. The stock market is a popular topic of conversation. Money is a topic.

*C.M.:What is the biggest threat to earning money?*

*M.J.:* Yourself: debt—digging such a big hole you can't get out of it. We were sent credit cards in college and we thought, "Free money!" We're still paying for that. It wasn't really free money.

*C.M.: Define success for your generation?*

*M.J.:* Being happy with who you are. And I think most people assign some sort of financial value to success. You've got to feel comfortable day in and day out doing what you're doing and being who you are.

*C.M.: How do you want your generation remembered?*

*M.J.:* Not materialistic. That we placed value on intangible things like morals and happiness. The attitude of: "I'm going to do what I want to, like it or not." Other generations may not respect that. But it's respectable. We're very individualistic.

*Subject:* **Erin M. Fuller, CAE**
*Age:* **33**
*Location:* **McLean, Virginia**
*Title:* **Executive Director**
*Employer:* **National Association of Women Business
  Owners (NAWBO)**

*Cam Marston:What is your generation's attitude today?*

*Erin Fuller:* An environment of uncertainty. Growing up in the 1980s, there was a constant threat of nuclear war. The *Challenger* explosion. The high level of divorce. Rapid inflation. Even today, we don't think Social Security will be around when we're ready to retire.

*C.M.:What do you think this comes from?*

*E.F.:* In the 1980s, we saw a lot of "Greed is good." We turned against that in the 1990s, and that's where the grunge movement came from. Today we don't believe that money itself is evil, but it is the means to achieve some sort of freedom—some sort of choice about your lifestyle. To the yuppie Baby Boomers, money was a means to amass the most toys. There isn't a label consciousness among Gen Xers. Money to Gen X means gaining freedom or access to freedom. And I don't think it's a phase. I think it's settling in for the long haul.

My parents' and grandparents' generations were very much into respect and loyalty for the corporation. Our generation doesn't believe that. We're very much aware of the trade we're giving our employers. I am happy to give you my time and energy in exchange for pay and respect for my ideas—but not *all* of my time and energy. We're very concerned about not burning out, not having failed relationships.

*C.M.: What incentives work for your generation?*

*E.F.:* Opportunity for personal growth and development. Opportunities to do things we haven't done before, to explore the unknown. Not as much compensation as the opportunity to learn a new skill. To me personally, having ownership in some cool new thing is important, although compensation is always good. I don't think people in our generation are as title conscious. With people older than I am it's important to use titles because it helps them figure out where I fit in the organization. To people my own age, though, I don't ever mention my title. They don't really care too much.

*C.M.: As a manager, how do you work with the people who report to you?*

*E.F.:* I manage Generation X. I try to give them a lot of personal recognition and praise, and when appropriate I give them small title changes. Their view of work goes something like this: "Work is where I am for this part of the day. Then I'm home for the rest of the day." My staff is more motivated by having a more comfortable office. I will present personalized gifts, like coupons for massages to a member of my staff who absolutely loves them. They're much better than a standard plaque or certificate where you just fill in the blank. If I know a certain staff member has a unique hobby, I make sure that the gift supports that.

*C.M.: Do you ever change the way you speak or the language that you use when dealing with members of different generations?*

*E.F.:* I used to. When I first went to work for a former employer, I was 15 years younger than the other vice presidents. So I had to monitor my "cool's." I am more comfortable now. I was thrilled when I finally hit 30. People don't dismiss me because I'm in my twenties anymore.

I now think my younger age works to my advantage, especially since I am in a role occupied by very few young women. I believe my age was actually refreshing compared to other candidates, and it worked to get me this job, although I had to fight against prejudices initially.

*C.M.: Do you think that those who are older than you expect you to show them deference for their seniority?*

*E.F.:* Absolutely. They want you to acknowledge that their years of experience in some way equate to wisdom, that they have greater knowledge or expertise than I do. I read it as a security thing.

There was a woman who came to my former employer as a new hire. She was probably 20 years older than me. When she introduced herself she said, "I have over 20 years in association management, so I'm sure that all of my experience will be a great resource to you." I instantly disliked *her*. I thought, "I don't care how long you've been working in the association business. What are you doing now?" Her attitude said, "I've done this a million times, so I know what will work and what won't."

*C.M.: What is the biggest incorrect stereotype of Gen X?*

*E.F.:* The whole slacker thing: the general idea that we don't want to work hard or that we were spoiled in our youth. The truth is that every generation thinks the generation following them doesn't have to work as hard. The truth is we're willing to work differently. The 70- or 80-hour workweek is not an effective life strategy. We were smart enough to figure that out. But we shouldn't be penalized for it.

*C.M · Are there stereotypes that fit?*

*E.F.:* There's always been this independence thing. We're not supposed to be joiners. I think that's true. For every generation, I think
there is some resource that is the ultimate goal. For the Baby
Boomers it was money. For us it is time. The time poverty we're experiencing has made us very, very selective over how we are going to
use it.

*C.M.: How important is it that you fit in your office?*

*E.F.:* One hundred percent. If I realize that I'm not a fit, I get the hell
out as soon as possible. If you dread going there because the environment is toxic then you're not a fit. If the environment drains your energy, if you don't trust the people you work with, if you have nothing
left by the end of the day, then get out. I need to work with people
who are smart workers and have a sense of humor about what they
do—people who realize that what they do is not brain surgery.

*C.M.: What about when you're interviewing people? How do you know
whether they'll fit or not?*

*E.F.:* I ask a lot of experiential questions, similar to "How do you
handle stress?" But I don't phrase it that way since it's such a cliché. I
try to create some sort of stressful situation and ask how they would
prioritize things or how they might have prioritized things in the
past. I want to know how they're responding to me. Do I feel like
I'm making a connection with them? I make interviewees take "the
beer test." It goes like this: "Are you willing to work with someone
all day, fight about ideas, not agree on anything, yet still be willing to
go out and drink beer with them after work?" If so, then there's a fit.
Humor is hugely important. A positive attitude is very important.

*C.M.: What is Generation X paranoid about?*

*E.F.:* Failure of relationships and general instability. People are very
cautious about the relationships they engage in. Even when they take
a job, they don't typically plunge in. They sit around the edges and

try to understand the lay of the land. Backgrounds may include failed relationships, so they're very cautious about entering into a relationship unless they're very comfortable with it.

*C.M.: How do you define success?*

*E.F.:* People who I think are successful are those who seem to be comfortable in their own skin—people who have achieved something great but it's not their exclusive focus; it's just one part of who they are.

*C.M.: What lessons did your parents' generation teach you about money?*

*E.F.:* Have it. Being the child of a single mother, I think it was very important for me to establish my own financial independence. And I wanted to do it before I got married. So I bought my own house. I have no school debt remaining. All of this was very important to me.

# 5

# The New Millennials

## *The Future of Our Workplace*

I've chosen to refer to the generation following Gen X into the workplace as the New Millennials for several reasons. The turn of the twenty-first century was one of the most anticipated events of recent memory, one that caused considerable concern as well—especially from a technological perspective. Y2K was a worldwide obsession for months. We all remember the dire predictions and enormous cost to many companies seeking the right technology fix. In retrospect, it's almost funny to think that the world waited, holding its breath, to see if civilization as we knew it would end.

Y2K, however, came in like a lamb, and, as we celebrated this momentous event, commentators pointed out how much everyone's lives had changed from 1900 to 2000: the differences a century makes. Here are just a few of them:

- Properly processed, safe foods are now mandated by law.
- Medical advances have added 30 to 40 years to the New Millennials' life expectancy, compared to the Matures'.
- International air (and space) travel, communications technology, and international commerce have given us a true global economy and a truly changing workplace.

But the obvious changes are not what really separate the young immigrants of the early 1900s, who were just starting out in their new country, from our New Millennials of today, just beginning their careers.

### The Unique World of the New Millennials (Or Other Things They Don't Remember)

- They study the 1960s as history, with no nostalgia.
- They have no memory of the Cold War.
- To them, *Leave It to Beaver* is a Discovery Channel show.
- Landing on the moon was what they did in the "olden days."
- AIDS has always existed.
- If you tell them that they sound like a broken record, they'll ask, "What's a record?"
- They don't remember Pac Man.
- They've never seen a TV without cable.
- *The Tonight Show* has always been hosted by Jay Leno.
- Popcorn eaten at home has always been cooked in the microwave.
- They don't know Mork or "De plane, de plane."
- They cannot answer the question, "Where's the beef?"

It's obvious that industrial, economic, and social advances over the past century account for part of the 180-degree change in attitude for the New Millennials. However, there is much more to the story of how we got from the millions who sought only steady work and freedom of expression to the millions who feel entitled to all of life's rewards without paying their dues.

The Millennials were raised during years of unique wealth in this country. Until the recent times of financial instability, they've known only comfort, if not outright prosperity. While older generations have always experienced hard times, the New Millennials are feeling it now, for the first time.

## The American Workplace

One of the most important changes over the past one hundred years is in the kind of work people do. In the early part of the twentieth century, the vast majority of Americans worked with their hands—in fields, in factories, or on assembly lines. In 1900, of the 29 million people in the workforce, 21.8 million of them did manual labor. For managers, at least until the past few decades, technology was not the critical factor it is today.

At the dawn of the twentieth century, a wave of European immigrants sought the promise of the American dream. The New Millennials are the greatest example of that dream coming true. The goal of a better life, one free from oppression and filled with opportunity, has been realized on many different levels for many people. Even though the dream has not yet been fulfilled for everyone, it is far more of a reality in the United States today than anywhere else.

The New Millennials have an extra gift—almost as if they were born with a new strand of DNA: They are the first entirely technologically savvy generation to enter the workplace. They do not know a time when calculators weren't used in math classes, reports weren't researched on the Internet, they didn't have a personal computer, and they were unable to talk to their friends on a cell phone or send instant messages, 24/7.

This new generation of entry-level workers is far different from the immigrants who acquired their skills as apprentices or by spending decades in an industrial environment. For those who made it up the ladder during the twentieth century, it was a hard-earned, lifelong struggle that was taken seriously and was all-consuming. The dawn of the New Millennium changed all that. Once the New Millennials fully join the workforce, Baby Boomers and Gen Xers will, once again, have to readjust the way they manage and conduct business.

Here's an example of what is already happening.

You are a Boomer. Assume you work at a large advertising agency. You've been at three agencies over 20 years and worked your way up. You are now the creative director and responsible for more than $100 million a year in business. You are always searching for "young, fresh, creative talent" with the emphasis on "talent." You've been given a new assignment—build a new creative unit to reach out to young people for a new clothing line. Your solution—one that has worked for you many times in the past—is to use peers of the target market to develop the campaign, and your boss bought into the idea. However, this is a cutthroat industry and, as always, your job is on the line.

After weeks of recruiting and three months of work, you are about to pull out what little hair you have because your workforce— all 29 of them are under 25 years old—is driving you crazy. You ask yourself: "Who are these kids?"

For one thing, 21 of them have just come into the workforce from college. They're in their first year of their first professional, career-type jobs. Yet clearly they're bored with their work, because it has already become routine to them.

Worse, the client bought—in fact loved—the campaign idea. The crew's reaction? They want promotions and all the perks they think should come with it—car allowances, more vacation, a pay raise. Heck, you don't have a company car!

You've even heard several of them say: "I'm overqualified for this job."

They tell you they want the perks that they think should come with success because of this one campaign. And they also hint that there might be another position out there for them if things don't work out in your department soon!

(If you want the truth, they're already pinging and instant messaging their friends to learn if there are openings in their companies, where they may do something a little different, earn a little more money, and work with their friends during the day.)

Personally, you think these kids don't have the experience to wash your noncompany, five-year-old car, much less deserve a promotion. You admire their confidence (verging on arrogance) and wish you had the chutzpah they have. And you know they can quit and be working again for someone else in a matter of days in another job across the street.

You wonder, yet again, what you're going to have to do to keep average entry-level New Millennial employees happy on the job, or you'll certainly lose them. They have little commitment to the company or to you. What are you going to do? All they seem to be concerned with is themselves and what job best suits them.

Rarely do I interview a Boomer who doesn't have a similar story and an opinion. While they admire the New Millennials' "go-get-it" and "why-not-me?" attitudes, they're somewhat taken aback by their brazen, self-accommodating approach. Here's another example.

The manager of a nursing unit at a hospital in Albany, Georgia, explained her view of the major differences in the generations in the workplace. She said that the Generation X and Millennial employees have clearly established what is "theirs" (the employees') and "ours" (the company's). For example, when she told some of her Gen X employees they would need to call in over the weekend to get their schedules for the upcoming week, they responded by saying, "The weekend is my time. Will I get paid an hour for the call?" She was dumbstruck.

She has more stories. Back when she had just started working as a nurse at the hospital, the shift supervisor invited everyone to go out for a drink after work, and she diligently went along. Though she was off the clock, she knew that going to the bar with the team after work was a part of her job. Truthfully, she said, she could have turned down the offer, but the repercussions, while certainly not fatal, would have harmed her in her career. She wouldn't have been considered a team player, and, as we've seen for Boomers, image is 90 percent of success. Going to the bar and spending time with other members of her team was part of her commitment to being successful—and it worked.

Today, when she invites her employees to go out for a beer after work, the Generation X and New Millennial employees rarely come. "That sounds like fun," they say, "but I already have plans. Let's do it some other time, and give me some advance notice." She's frustrated. She wants to build a team among her employees, and the younger generations have no desire to put in time forging the team bonds outside of the office.

It cannot be overemphasized that technology has radically changed the New Millennials' world. Though Gen X and the Boomers have seen technology alter the workplace, New Millennials have lived during a time when technological advances are measured in half-lives. For them, technology is a part of life, an extension of their arms and minds, not just a tool used to find the solution. It is virtually assured that technology will continue to change and evolve faster than it already has thus far simply because those who know it best—the New Millennials—are driving it.

Like some of Generation X, the majority of New Millennials were brought up by parents who wanted their children to be their friends. It is the parents of the Millennials who say, "My daughter is my best friend." Again, the focus on quality time, not parenting time, created the kind of friendship between parent and child that didn't exist when Boomers where children. And like the Xers, many New Millennials say they need role models in their lives—they have enough friends.

For many reasons, explained in dozens of other books, the parents of the New Millennials—mostly Boomers—became obsessed with their children. Parents' lives revolved around taking their children to practices, to and from school, and on trips designed to broaden their horizons. The children were not a blessed by-product of a marriage; they were the nucleus of the marriage, and they grew up showered with attention. While the concept of soccer moms has been the butt of late-night TV jokes, they weren't funny to marketers or politicians, who coveted the spending power and votes of these women.

Their parenting style was different, too. Political correctness and education came into the home on a level not seen before. Experts suggested that children not be punished and certainly never spanked. Rather, they should be told that feeding the goldfish to the cat was "not a good choice."

When, as young children, they asked "Why?" (Why is the sun bright? Why does the car make a loud noise? Why is it raining?), their parents assiduously attempted to explain the reason behind each of these phenomena. The "teachable moment" was the response to every question as information was downloaded by Baby Boomers to enable their children to better compete in the future. Employers today will tell you that New Millennials have never stopped asking those questions and never lowered their expectations that answers are forthcoming.

Self-esteem was another major focus, and it has played into the attitude that the New Millennials bring to the workplace. Boomer parents raised their children by building their egos.

- As young children, the Millennials played soccer, and everyone on the team was given a chance to score a goal. The final score wasn't kept because every child on the field was "a winner."
- Children either excelled in school or were "special learners."
- Children who had trouble focusing or being quiet were diagnosed with a new disease—attention deficit disorder (ADD), which was treated with prescription medication.

Rarely was a child's bad behavior the fault of the child or the parents' involvement (or lack thereof). There was always something else at the root of the problem—the decay of social norms, too heavy an influence by the media, and other societal factors. In other words, the child was never wrong.

Remember "Baby on Board"? From the rear windows of minivans, station wagons, and SUVs hung the bright yellow placard that called out to anyone nearby, "Precious cargo! Be careful! Stay away!"

Today, those babies are entering your workplace.

## In the Workplace

Another unique factor distinguishes the New Millennials: many of them have been able to extend their adolescence by 10 years. They're living at home longer—60 percent of college students said they planned to move home after graduation. They're marrying later, buying homes later, bearing children later, and staying in school longer. They're not facing the same pressures (or desires) as their parents did to get their own homes and become self-sufficient by finding a job and going to work. As a result, many of their forays into the workplace are experimental: "Do I like this?" " Is this fun?" " Is this what I want to do?" They feel less pressure to select a career in their twenties or, in some cases, even at all.

When the New Millennials' Boomer parents completed their schooling, whether it was high school, college, or postgraduate work, their parents expected them to "Go out and get a job." Essentially, they said, "You're on your own now."

Those same Boomers, now parents of the New Millennials, are saying to their children, "Go out and find a good job that makes you happy." The difference? Self-sufficiency versus self-fulfillment.

While the Boomers hoped to find fulfillment after they began their careers, either by working toward it or stumbling onto it, New Millennials, with the encouragement of their parents, are searching for fulfillment first. Afterwards they'll work toward self-sufficiency. And self-fulfillment is rarely to be achieved in the workplace for New Millennials—it is found outside the workplace. The job is simply the way they can afford whatever their self-fulfillment is—hiking, travel, social schedules, and other nonwork activities.

New Millennials are more aware than any of the previous generations that guarantees no longer exist in the workplace. A good education doesn't guarantee a job, and a job doesn't guarantee long-term employment. Everything about the workplace is tentative. "Will I be here next week? Will this company be here next week? Will my boss be here next week?" They are a generation that mirrors General Electric CEO Jack Welch's statement, "At the end of the week I'll pay you for the work you've done. We're square, even. Monday we start again." They are selling you their time. And they're good with that.

Having been raised by parents who continually bolstered their egos, New Millennials begin working with tremendous goals for themselves. They have high aspirations and every intention of reaching them. They know what they want to do and where they want to be, but they have no idea how to get there, mostly because they lack sufficient experience to create the blueprint that will get them from where they are today to their goals. And that is where their bosses come into the picture.

Like Gen Xers, New Millennials have changed the definition of loyalty yet again. Their loyalty is often to the person for whom they work, because that person is leading them to their goals and is helping them construct the road map that will get them where they want to go. Past generations have had to create this path on their own. But New Millennials relied on their parents to do it, and now, in the workplace, they're relying on their bosses, their substitute parents, to help them. Like Gen Xers, they're loyal to people, not to companies.

*When New Millennials decide to leave, they don't quit the company; they quit the boss. If the boss isn't helping them get where they want to go, they're off.*

### New Millennials—Who Will They Be in the Future?

Do the attitudes and behaviors of New Millennials reflect their youthfulness or their generational personality? Will these characteristics change as they grow up, or will they persist throughout their lives?

A good part of their attitudes is a reflection of their extended adolescence—they remain almost-grown children much longer. And because they believe, as young people always have, that they are indestructible, they may think, "With the potential for advancements in science that exists now, I'm going to be a functional,

healthy person until I'm a hundred years old. Why rush to work?"
It makes sense. Eventually, though, they will experience more of
the world, and the facts of life and aging will produce a more
grounded outlook.

But certain generational characteristics will very likely remain—
balance, a sense of entitlement, a life outside of work, and valuing
time with their friends, among others. Time will tell if these are indeed generational characteristics.

---

### The Workplace Snapshot

- In the past, Baby Boomers defined work ethic by
  how many hours they put in at work. If you worked
  a 60-hour week, you were on the right track and a
  hard worker; you had a bright future.

- Today, Generation X and New Millennials often measure an
  effective work ethic by whether they get their jobs done on
  time, not by how many hours they work each week. They
  are as likely to perceive even office social gatherings and hol-
  iday parties as intrusions on their time rather than rewards
  for performance.

- Gen Xers and New Millennials know more about the technology that drives almost all businesses and can use it with
  ease. Technology to them is a freedom tool. It enables them
  to complete their jobs faster and more easily, so they
  can get back to what's important—their lives outside of the
  office.

- For Gen Xers and New Millennials, titles and promotions
  are interesting by-products of work, not motivations to work
  harder.

- Gen Xers are cynical about meetings and view them largely as posturing sessions full of hooey. Boomers, though, use them as a way to measure progress and build consent.

- How do you create teams to accomplish a task when there are three generations, each essentially speaking a different language?

- How do you create teams when Generation X and New Millennials are more interested in how they'll benefit from being on the team than in team spirit? Isn't personal benefit an inherent contradiction of what a team is about?

- Boomers don't like teams but know they are necessary to successful achievement of workplace goals. Boomers also know that their performance on the team is important to their own success. Gen Xers don't much care for teams, so they try to make them as much fun as possible, with rotating leadership and different meeting locations and hours.

- Work must not, and cannot, be fun to Boomers; it's serious. It is their life. If work is fun, something is wrong.

- Gen Xers say, "Get a life." New Millennials say, "I have a life. Work comes second."

It is a fact that in the twenty-first-century workplace success is measured differently by different generations.

## "I Don't Want Your Life"

Meet Jane, who is the human resources manager for a large multinational company headquartered in Washington, D.C. Each year, she can be found traveling across the country organizing and directing the HR functions in eight or ten major divisions of the company. Each division has several thousand employees. She's in her midforties and unmarried. Typical of Boomers, she works long hours and usually brings work home with her; in fact, she can't remember a day when she has not taken a full briefcase home.

Recently she returned from a business trip to find that one of her young and highly skilled assistants had resigned abruptly. When asked for a reason, Jane was shocked to hear him say, "I watch how hard you work and I don't want that kind of life."

And worse, Jane was crushed not just because she had lost a good employee but because his observation was so valid. It was true—she worked all the time. And, she admitted, she had no idea how to change. It was her lifestyle, and it was her life. In order to be successful, Jane believed, she had to work to the exclusion of almost everything else.

It is clear that understanding each generation's point of view is crucial to successful management across generations. How ironic is it that one generation's idea of success is rejected as nonsuccess according to another generation's point of view?

Did Baby Boomers arrive at this unique point of view because they suddenly realized that they are their parents' age? By and large, they embraced their parents' work ethic. The good old counterculture disappeared as they grew up. Even though young employees in today's workforce are their children's age, the Baby Boomers report that they don't feel old, especially not the way Jane's employee viewed her. While the Boomers did want to surpass their parents' success, the new workforce does not want to reach Boomers' age and be like the Boomers—meaning they want to maintain their separate values. It is a quandary for the Boomers, who still listen to rock music, party, climb mountains, and even have sex just like the younger generation!

For Boomers, the definition of success is clear and unambiguous:

- My father considers himself successful because he worked hard to create a dental practice with loyal patients and staff. He fed and clothed his family all the while. His definition of success comes from years of effort. He is successful because his hard work paid off.

- Jane is successful, too. She works long and hard to make the best meetings and events that she is capable of, and she does it time and time again. Her hard work is a critical part of her success. When asked what motivates her, she knows exactly what to answer. When people come to her who know how hard she has worked and thank her for her efforts, she has succeeded.

Is it that simple—that success is measured differently by different generations?

Let's look at some other stories that explore how Boomers react to Gen X and New Millennial employees and how Boomers approach the age/generation quandary in their dual roles that include direct responsibilities and their managerial function.

## What Happened to Sacrifice?

Sheila, a Baby Boomer, is a vice president at a medium-sized bank whom I have known for many years. She's a complete professional: She carries herself with confidence, looks you right in the eye when she talks to you, is very organized, and knows her business backward and forward. Everything about her exudes confidence, from the firm handshake to the nicely tailored suits to the artwork in her neat and tidy office. Not long after she opened my first checking account years ago, she was recruited to a small, high-end local bank.

In order to succeed, Sheila had to slow the constant exodus of employees and make her branch operate like clockwork. She assessed the situation and solved it using both her management and her leadership skills. Not long after that, her success led to another job running a main bank branch in a key city location. In the two years she has been there, she has turned this branch around, too. By her own account, she works hard and expects a lot from herself.

But the situation she now faces is more difficult. She used to be able to expect a lot from her employees. Now she has had to lower her expectations.

This is what she told me:

> My biggest problem today and most consistent headaches come from dealing with employee problems—the biggest of which is apathy.
>
> The tellers don't care if they don't balance out at the end of the day, the loan officers don't care if they win the loan, and the customer service agents don't care if they're able to answer the customers' questions or not.
>
> I call it a generational malaise. As hard as I work to keep my employees happy, none seem to be devoted to the job or to the company or even to improving their own skills to get a raise. Every day, I work harder and harder just to get an average employee to do the minimum job.
>
> When I first started, I rarely spoke to my boss about anything but work-related matters.
>
> I don't expect praise from anyone. I just want to do my job well, and I don't want acclaim simply for doing the minimum.
>
> Today, I have to acknowledge my employees for doing the minimal amount of work or I won't even get the minimum. When I was a new employee, the management style was, "If you don't hear from me, assume you're doing well."
>
> If I don't speak with the employees or chat with them, they simply don't perform. They need the chatter, the feedback, the relationship (real or perceived) with their boss.

Sheila is successful, having repeatedly transformed bank branches from chaos to seamless organizations. She says that for her, it is enough that her peers know of her successes, as do her superiors.

But for each of these individuals' successes, what has been the cost—what opportunity has been lost? Is it possible that Generation X and the even younger New Millennials have identified what was lost and decided that they won't make those sacrifices themselves?

How do the kids see things? The answer will surprise most Baby

Boomers. In fact, more than we care to admit, their view of Boomers is accurate. But their view of their own work future is shortsighted. Or is it?

Let's return to my conversation with Sheila:

> I have a little girl in the eighth grade. She's a super student. First, she's quite bright, and second, she works hard at school. She'll do well in high school and college. Every now and then she comes downstairs looking tired before school and I ask her how she feels. She'll say she's tired or doesn't want to go to school today for whatever reason, and every now and then when this happens, she and I will take "sick days" and spend the day together. We call them sick days because we're both sick of our jobs—hers is school and mine is at the bank. So we just take a day for ourselves and shop, watch movies, and spend time together. It is nice. We don't do it often, so those days are special for us. Besides, she's a good student and gets good grades, so it's okay.

This is the same Sheila who was complaining that her Gen X and Millennial employees don't come to work from time to time. They take fake sick days and return to work the next day looking refreshed and relaxed, with a new sport coat, a new pair of shoes, or a new manicure. And Sheila gets upset at them for not wanting to work and being openly dishonest—as she should—but is Sheila teaching her daughter anything different? Is she leading by example? Or will Sheila's daughter enter the workforce in 10 years and, after she's worked hard for a while and begins feeling tired, take a "sick day" the way her mother taught her to do? What if Sheila's daughter is a good, hardworking employee? Will she be more likely or less likely to take fake sick days? According to Sheila's rationalizing, she'll take more.

## Case History: Testimony from a Consultant and a Parent of New Millennials

I spoke to a colleague who was involved as a consultant in a variety of media activities. His clients flew him around the United States and to Canada producing radio shows and packaging and publishing books. His career spanned three decades as a corporate vice president and a manager in four very large media companies, two of them international. He had been working on his career literally since age 10, and, like every other Baby Boomer manager, he had fought his way to the top by putting in the long hours and expertly learning his craft. This enabled him to offer his services as a consultant when his industry consolidated, and he took, as he called it, a "mental health package." He headed for the golf course at age 48.

Six months later, he was bored and ready to go back to work. But his personal life, like that of many of his colleagues, had gotten rough around the edges during the run to the top. He'd developed health problems and, like approximately half of his friends, had a marriage that was teetering, if not toppled. Plus, he had two expensive college tuitions to fund, a vastly reduced income, no company car, and no fun perks. The 1990s were definitely over.

Fortunately, he'd been very careful to keep up with technology and its effect on his business—especially the Internet and the power of a web site to act as a virtual direct-marketing site and even a one-to-one cyber-resume post. Although he couldn't do what the kids did—write code or manipulate a Mac's design functions—he knew how they did what they did, and how to ask for what he wanted or envisioned. As the technology to develop a web site evolved from a cost of hundreds of thousands of dollars to needing only off-the-shelf software, he was careful to keep up.

About the time he opted out of the corporate world, Gen X had appeared on the scene. His overall impression was that most of them couldn't read or write a coherent sentence. They were not really driven, and basically he thought they were the product of a failed education system. His own children, who were part of the New Millennial generation, seemed fairly typical of their generation—more interested in computer games than in books, even though both their parents were in the media.

In hindsight, he realized that his kids had been around computers—basically word processors and then PCs—most of their lives, and so had the majority of their friends. Further, he found out that virtually every school library had computer terminals, and students were now required to use complicated graphing calculators in math class. Whatever happened to good old equations and slide rules? Clearly, this was a major difference between the generations.

Five years later, both kids are out of school. They are full-fledged New Millennials, equipped from head to toe with cell phones, laptops, DVD burners, and iPods. One is an attorney, a 26-year-old with a prestigious one-year judicial clerkship. The other is a 22-year-old seeking an entry-level media job. Unfortunately for Dad, by now the full force of the New Millennials in the workplace has hit, and as he consults at various companies he encounters more and more clones of his own kids attaining positions of responsibility.

He has noticed there is not a general stereotype that fits them. While they all have either ill-defined goals or very strongly defined ambition, their personal circumstances drive their job behaviors.

For example, he was hired by a small family-owned company to assist with new product development. Once he arrived, he recognized that one of the major problems was organization. This, in turn, prevented new product development and revenue growth. The employees were all under 30—Gen Xers or New Millennials. The only people over 30 were the owner/partners, a husband-and-wife team, aged 57 and 60, respectively.

The company was run in a trickle-down manner. The boss, who was a member of the Matures, more or less told people what he wanted done. He held lengthy, informal, conference-room lunch meetings and "kind of talked out what he wanted." The result was that the company was doing well, but it was run like an extended family.

As a trained Baby Boomer–era manager, the consultant's first thought was classic: Institute a reorganization. Make the company work more efficiently and institute a decentralized management system. For the first time, employees actually were given job descriptions and titles. A clearly superior employee assumed the number two spot below the owner to run the company day to day.

Two things happened. One surprised our consultant and one did not. He knew from his own professional and personal experiences that the younger Gen Xers in the company would jump in with both feet. They now had clearly defined jobs, roles, and lines of communication that enabled them to get their work done effectively, especially since most of them were very computer savvy. If they needed a day off to go to a soccer game, they knew whom to ask and didn't feel as if the "plantation boss" was doing them a favor. However, they'd have to repay the time off with compensatory time later on.

What surprised him most (but in retrospect should not have) was that the boss was unable to adjust easily. As the new system went into effect and the company revenues rose, he became resentful. With nothing to really complain about, he directed his unhappiness toward the consultant, shooting down his ideas and suggestions. The Gen Xers and New Millennials on the staff, however, were ecstatic and their productivity rose substantially. Within a year, the company had doubled in size, and five years later it was stronger and larger than anyone could have imagined. The boss, as a Mature, surrendered to age and health issues. He took the golf course semiretirement route and retained final say only on large expenditures.

The experience was a valuable one for our consultant, who worked there for two years before moving on to a new project. First, he recognized that some time-tested Baby Boomer management techniques worked—especially with the Gen X group—but only if applied in a certain manner. For example, decentralizing, making responsibility clear, and injecting some flexibility into a rigid system made for a happy workplace.

But he also learned that if management was not fully on board with a Gen X/New Millennial–oriented management system, it would be hard to install. This is the real problem in overcoming the generational divide—deciding who will be the one to give in first.

In determining which generation has more leverage in the workplace, the answer is not as simple as who has the most authority. The reality is that the future is technology-based, no matter what industry you point to. Technology will save you money, increase your profits, make your business more efficient, and help you keep up with the competition. Gen Xers and New Millennials have always known a cyber-technological world, whether it was Nintendo or a turbocharged PC. Many computer-savvy younger people build their own computers just because they can. And many, many kids in college today know how to create a web site. They text message each other continually and are eager to embrace everything new.

As for Boomers, our consultant says, "I think what I've learned is that the advice of one of my old mentors was the best: 'Surround yourself with people who are smarter than you are, and let them do their thing and make you look good!'"

## Generational Voice

*Subject:* **Anonymous**
*Age:* **New Millennial**

*Cam Marston: Who are your heroes?*

*Anonymous:* I think that's the hardest question. Since September 11 people in the armed forces and in the fire department come to my mind first. But as for members of my generation, I can't think of anyone.

*C.M.: How is your generation stereotyped?*

*Anon.:* We're stereotyped as being lazy, as if things were handed to us on a silver platter. We've lost the work ethic; we're driven by money and expectant of money and materialistic things. I don't agree with the stereotypes, but I think that they are correct. I always tell my dad I can't imagine how my grandchildren will live, because I don't see it getting any better than it is right now.

*C.M.: Is it important that you fit in your office?*

*Anon.:* I definitely think it's important to fit. You either fit there or you don't. You know right away whether someone fits.

*C.M.: When you work with someone you like, what are their characteristics?*

*Anon.:* Communication is really, really important to me: being quick to admit a mistake and quick to ask for help; being up front and direct with problems.

*C.M.: What is your generation paranoid about?*

*Anon.:* They fear getting worse than they are, regarding selfishness, motivation, and how the people in my generation expect things to be handed to them. They worry about war. Are we economically safe? What's the money market going to be like in 20 years?

*C.M.: What is success to you?*

*Anon.:* Success is very much on a personal level. I am very work driven. I am very end-result driven. I like tangible end results.

*C.M.: What will a life of success look like?*

*Anon.:* After 80 years, success for me will be more of looking at my personal life. What kind of person have I been? Who have I been involved with? My friends and my family. To be happy in my job. My heart dedicated to what I'm doing.

# 6

## Why Work?

### *The Generational Divide Surfaces in the Workplace*

Has this ever happened to you?

You're a Boomer boss. One morning a new employee approaches you in your office. This person is under 25 years old. Whether he or she is college educated is unimportant. Race and gender are unimportant. Rural or urban lifestyle, again, is unimportant. This employee sincerely asks you, "Boss, what do I need to know to be the best employee I can be for you? What skills are necessary for me to perform well for the company and for you?"

You think to yourself, "Wow. What a great question. I wish they'd all ask me this, so I don't have to spend so much time trying to teach the answers."

You tell this person that anyone who accepts and follows four key suggestions will do quite well anywhere.

1. Develop a work ethic. A work ethic is necessary for success, and having a good, strong work ethic means working long and hard at your job. It means hours and effort. No one who is successful today got there without a good work ethic.
2. You'll need to know how to fit in and operate as part of a team. Teams are the nucleus of success. The team's efforts su-

persede your own, and once you learn to function in a team you'll be positioned to lead that team and take on new levels of responsibility.

3. Acquire patience and be willing to sacrifice. There will be a time when you'll be impatient for a promotion or to see your work yield results; that's when a good understanding of the value of patience is necessary because it will pay off in the end. Nothing good comes quickly. You'll be asked to make some sacrifices for the company that will interfere with your life outside of work, your vacation, and maybe your family, but those sacrifices are necessary to be successful. Everyone here has sacrificed a lot for this company.

4. You'll need to understand what it means to pay your dues—waiting your turn for promotions, bonuses, and raises. It means taking the lowest-level jobs and doing them anyway until you've paid your dues and someone else comes along who will take over those jobs. Anyone who has been success-ful has had to pay their dues along the way.

There might be a lot more advice of this kind. To a typical Boomer in today's workplace, the list of attributes necessary for suc-cess is long.

Here's what I mean by "the generational divide." In the unlikely event that this scenario actually played out, a Boomer would quickly discover that Gen Xers and New Millennials can barely relate to these values. Their life experiences have only rarely, if ever, made it necessary to practice these attributes in order to sur-vive in a competitive environment. Is it possible these values and behaviors are simply foreign to them? Is the Boomer boss in this scenario speaking the same language as the young employee asking the question, or is he speaking a foreign tongue—you might call it "Boomerese"?

In truth, the employee's Boomer parents have already laid out the message of strong work ethic, team playing, and paying dues, but that doesn't mean the child of a Boomer actually believes the message. Gen Xers and New Millennials wonder whether it is really necessary to undergo so much stress and self-denial to be successful. They've witnessed the turmoil in their parents' lives, and some of them think these values and work habits are actually *harmful* to success.

In fact, there may be whole new definitions of the word *success* that are alive, well, and operational in the workplace, and the leaders of today's workplace are unaware of them. They're plugging away assuming that if they wait it out long enough, younger generations will ultimately grow up. But they're sadly mistaken. Each generation uses the word *success* differently. And while the Boomers undoubtedly know what it takes to be successful, they're using the word from their own point of view and are assuming that all their employees have a similar definition.

## Why Work?

One fundamental question asked by Gen Xers and New Millennials is very simple: "Why work?" The question is really about motivation. For Boomers, the answer is obvious: Work pays you an income, and with that income you pay for the items you need to stay alive. The motivation of later generations is less transparent. Let's review the fundamental differences.

### *The Boomers*

We know that Baby Boomers define themselves by their work. Imagine you, a Boomer, run into a friend at the shopping center one day. Your friend is with a companion you have never met before. You shake hands with the companion, and he says to you: "Tell me all about yourself." For a typical Baby Boomer the answer might be, "My name is Jim, and I'm an engineer at XYZ Products." What stands out here?

- The name comes first—it is the most important information for anyone to disclose upon meeting another person. Unique to the Boomers, though, is the second part of the answer—the self-definition as an income earner. It is such a significant part of the way Boomers see themselves that it immediately follows the name in an introduction. Members of no other generation except Boomers define themselves by their jobs.
- Another Boomer goal is to make a difference at work. Boomers are inspired to make positive change around them, and they find it fulfilling when they do. Of course, any generation enjoys rewards from knowing that they have made improvements, but for Boomers it's often a driving focus.
- Baby Boomers tend to work out of loyalty to a company even though most of them realize that loyalty is dead and has been dead for a long time. Nevertheless, many Boomers remain loyal to their employers and continue to work because of that loyalty. Even though they know they could be axed from the payrolls at any moment, the old habits of allegiance are hard to break.

### Gen X

Generation X's reasons for working are different.

- Like Boomers, they work to pay the bills.
- An Xer works to learn new skills that will be of benefit either for working at the current job or to help toward getting the next one.
- Gen Xers assume there will be a next job. It's inevitable that they'll either get laid off or decide to move to another com-

pany. So Gen Xers prepare for this transition by learning as much as possible not only about technology but also about managerial practices that require them to learn a new skill set. Each new skill set a Gen Xer acquires creates another opportunity for the future. In their experience, a comprehensive skill base is more important to finding and landing the next job than Baby Boomers' beloved work ethic.

- Gen X works out of loyalty to people, not to the company, but only when their supervisors are superb communicators and motivators and know their employees well. When a Gen Xer finds a mentor, loyalty follows close behind.

### New Millennials

The New Millennials' reasons for working are different still:

- Now at the entry level of the workforce, New Millennials work so they can afford the lifestyles they want and earn enough money to pay for their hobbies. Work is a means to an end; it is not an end in itself.
- New Millennials, however, enjoy the social interactions among the groups of people with whom they work.
- They want the education they can get on the job.
- Much like Generation X, New Millennials are loyal not to the company, but rather to the person for whom they are working. Again like Generation X, New Millennials are searching for the boss who will lead them, not dictate to them. As children they were told by their teachers, by their parents, even by Burt and Ernie, that they could be whatever they wanted to be. Now, in and out of the workplace, New Millennials try to find the person who will help them achieve their goals in life, which might be attaining a position within the current company or moving into a completely different profession outside the company. Like the Generation Xers, if

a great boss, someone who has proven to be a good leader, were to leave the company, a New Millennial might attempt to go, too. The relationship with that person is more important than the relationship with the company.

### Hierarchical Style: Is It No Longer in Fashion?

In the 1990s, *work style* became a catchphrase to describe some of the more superficial changes in the workplace. For example, what started as "casual day" became "all-casual" or "smart-casual," giving rise to very successful stores like Banana Republic. Style, where management across the generations is concerned, is much more important than jeans versus khakis.

Baby Boomers inherited a workplace steeped in hierarchical style from their predecessors, the Matures. It was a buttoned-down style—ruled from the top down. While Boomers ultimately modified the hierarchy, they left quite a bit of it intact. There are protocols that must be obeyed. There are ways of doing things that have been in place for years and, though no one knows why they exist, they're still followed. Ironically, it was the Boomers who rallied in the streets in the 1960s against all the hierarchies then in control of society. Now they're complaining that today's kids don't show enough respect for these grand old institutions.

Gen Xers and New Millennials probably never encounter the term *hierarchical structure* until they begin to work for a company where a hierarchy is in place. Many of these new employees call their parents by their first names. Terms of address such as "ma'am" and "sir" have largely disappeared. E-mail has created an abbreviated form of the English language (LOL = laugh out loud; PITR = parent in the room; and so on). Even the White House web site offers an e-mail address for the president of the United States. (Imagine: "Hey Prez, 'Sup? Saw your speech. LOL. But can't write what I really think—PITR.")

Gen Xers and New Millennials, somewhat pessimistic and cynical already, automatically question authority figures in the workplace.

The reason is that during Xers' lifetimes, there has scarcely been a national authority figure who has not been exposed for lying or corruption. Consider the presidencies they've witnessed. Their earliest memories may be of Richard Nixon saying, "I am not a crook," followed by public impeachment hearings and his resignation in disgrace. And then there was the Reagan administration, tarnished by the Iran-Contra deals. And it will be hard to forget the Clinton administration, with the president proclaiming, "I did not have sexual relations with that woman, Ms. Lewinsky."

Generation X has witnessed enough lying to question leadership at every level, especially in business. They know that captains of one industry after another attempt to maintain public images of upright behavior while they are cheating their stockholders and their employees, and their empires implode (think Enron, WorldCom, Health-South, and many others). Gen X knows that countless workers who toiled for years and were loyal to their companies have been ruined, their retirement funds evaporated.

Consequently, when Gen Xers enter the workplace, they are especially wary of and resistant to hierarchy and authority. "What are they hiding?" they wonder to themselves.

## Testing, Testing . . .

It is common for a Gen Xer to test people in leadership positions. Generation X knows that words and behavior are often different, and that behavior is what truly matters, so they find ways to challenge their authority figures to see who they really are.

The bottom line for a Gen Xer is: "Do they do what they say and say what they do? Are they truthful? Can I rely on them to tell the truth all the time, or is this a smoke-and-mirrors game?" Once an authority figure has proven him- or herself to be genuine, Xers will follow where he or she leads them. The New Millennials feel the same way—they want to know if their leaders are true and whether they're truly leaders.

For Gen Xers and Millennials, company hierarchy is a barrier to the discovery process. In a workplace that relies heavily on hierarchy, with little access to the managers and officers in the company, Gen Xers and New Millennials believe that something is being hidden from them, or that the people at the top are untrustworthy. Workplaces that rely less heavily on hierarchy enable all the employees to get to know the people they work for. Because Gen Xers and New Millennials are loyal to individual people, not to companies, they need access to the people for whom they work. Access enables these younger employees to decide for themselves whether their bosses are trustworthy and will follow through on what they say. If so, the young employees will commit to loyalty.

### Is It Quitting Time Yet?

No single issue divides Boomers from Gen Xers and New Millennials more than the way time spent on the job is measured and valued.

We know that Boomers most often measure their loyalty and dedication to a company by the number of hours put in over the course of a day/week/month. In their minds, success equals hours spent at work. Oddly enough, actual productivity achieved during those hours is not an issue.

Battle lines between the generations are sometimes drawn over how much time it should actually take to *accomplish* the job. Generation X and New Millennials believe that the less time spent to get the job done right, the better—"If I get my job done on time and to the boss's satisfaction, I should be able to leave." The Gen Xers and New Millennials view long hours as inefficient and unnecessary if the job can be completed during normal business hours.

The younger employees want to know, "Are you paying me to be here or are you paying me to get the job done? Why does it matter where and how long I work as long as I get the job done?" Certainly, there are jobs where the actual presence of an employee in a specific place at a specific time is part of the job description—bank tellers, hotel clerks, and department store salespersons are only a few.

When I was a new employee in my first corporate job, my boss stopped by my cubicle late one Thursday afternoon. He looked troubled, as if he had something to say that made him uncomfortable. It was getting close to five o'clock, and, being a typical Gen Xer, I was organizing my things to leave for the day.

My boss said, "I'm tired."

"Really? Why?" I asked.

He replied, "I was here late last night, until about eight o'clock. I'll probably be here late tonight, too, and I expect I'll need to come in on Saturday or Sunday just to get everything done." And he gave me a look that I didn't understand at the time. He held my gaze a moment or two too long and then walked away.

Today I understand completely what he was trying to say. He was telling me that if I wanted to be on the team for that workplace, I needed to spend more time in the office, to work harder by staying late and coming in on the weekends. But his message flew right over my head.

To this day I remember myself thinking, "What is wrong with this guy that he can't get his work done during the normal business day? He needs some time management classes or something. Doesn't he have a life that he needs to get to? In fact, maybe he should be working for me since I don't have problems getting everything done that I need to over the course of a normal workday." Needless to say, I didn't last there long.

But when the work can be done at any time from any location, Gen Xers and New Millennials question the validity of strict working hours and the necessity of working long and hard to be "successful"—that is, to actually finish the job.

Here's another test: Ask a Gen Xer or New Millennial if he or she has a strong work ethic, and typically there is no clear answer. These employees know they don't fit the Baby Boomer definition of hard working employees, but they also know that they get their jobs done on time. So, even though they may not have a strong work ethic measured in Boomers' terms, they definitely have an *effective* work ethic.

### Productivity versus Work Ethic, or "Look Busy!"

Generation X and New Millennials will almost always cite productivity, not time spent working, as a standard of measurement for the work done. This is a deep source of frustration to many of their Boomer bosses, who don't necessarily cite productivity as a requirement when evaluating performance for rewards (bonuses, promotions, raises). Obviously Generation X and New Millennials feel that productivity should be the determinant for that type of workplace success and the rewards that are due.

Younger employees ask, "So what if they've been here longer? So what if they work longer? What are they actually doing with their time that makes them less productive than me? I get more done in less time. I work smarter. I use technology to my benefit. They don't even know how to use the technology! And they're being rewarded for getting less done in more time. That's not right!"

Boomers, you've got to face the facts: Generation X and New Millennials work smart during the day so that they can complete the job on time and get back to their lives. To them, the workplace isn't the definition of who they are; it is where they earn the money that makes their lifestyles affordable. And if they can do the job at odd hours and get it done to the satisfaction of their superiors, super. They shouldn't be restricted to the typical 8-to-5 workday. Likewise, if they can finish their job early to the satisfaction of their superiors, the remainder of the day should be theirs.

### Time to Get with the Program

Can Boomers live with this?

Many Boomers would have loved to work just the way Xers and New Millennials do. But such behavior, however efficient in terms of real accomplishment, would have made them appear unmotivated to their superiors. They wouldn't have been considered good team members. And this is where the real rift begins.

I remember another instance where the different generational attitudes toward time on the job became an issue. As a teenager, one of my first summer jobs was at a small local college in Mobile, Alabama, working on the grounds crew. Every day I'd arrive at work, and a map of the campus would be waiting for me. Highlighted on the map would be an outline of the area where I was to cut the grass that day. I'd take my mower, my fuel, my weeder, and other accessories and get to work. Typically, each job lasted about eight hours; then I'd go back to the office, clean up, and prepare the equipment for the next day. My father would pick me up just after 4:30 every afternoon to take me home.

One day I finished my cutting earlier than usual, returned to the shop, cleaned up, and called my father. "Dad," I said, "can you come get me?"

"What time is it?" he asked.

"Three-thirty."

"Don't you work until four-thirty?" he asked.

"Usually, yes. But I finished early today. Can you come get me?"

"I can, but you're not finished until four-thirty."

"No, you don't understand. I am finished. I cut the area they asked me to cut and I am ready to go."

"You can't be ready to go until four-thirty," he said.

"But I'm finished," I said, becoming frustrated.

*(Continued)*

"No you're not," he said, getting frustrated himself.

"Well, then, what am I supposed to do around here for another hour? I did everything they asked me to do today and I'm ready for tomorrow."

I still remember what he said: "Look busy."

I believed my employer was paying me to get the job done. I had completed the job; therefore, I was done for the day. My father believed, as do many people of his generation, that I needed to be seen there until quitting time, and that I was being paid to be there until that time.

Boomers think to themselves, "This is the way I had to do it. Therefore, this is the way you should do it. You have to follow my path into this workplace just the way I had to follow the path laid out for me." And Generation X and the New Millennials are saying, "No, thank you," and doing something different.

These profound differences exist in workplaces everywhere today. The result? Conflict—and lots of it.

In truth, there are two younger generations who define success differently. That means their path to success is different. Time is a shared, major component of success for all the generations currently in the workplace, but time is valued very differently by the older and younger groups. To the Boomers and Matures, time was something they had to invest in their careers. They became workaholics because they invested their extra time back into their work. To them, time is/was cheap, and giving it back to an employer through long hours of work was expected. To Gen Xers and New Millennials, time is expensive and needs to be controlled as closely and as tightly as money itself. Time has become a very real currency, just like dollars themselves, and giving control of it to the workplace is definitely not a part of a plan to become successful.

# 7

# If It's to Be, It's Up to Me

## *Be a Better Boss in the Twenty-First-Century Workplace*

Everyone knows that in storytelling (and in movies, too), point of view is everything. Clearly, each of the three generations now acting, interacting, and reacting in the workplace—as well as the retiring Matures—has a different point of view. As a manager across the generational divide, it's critical that you understand how each group sees things, which is what I've been discussing in the last few chapters.

### New Rules

Now you must confront the fact that when you're working for a company, whether it's your own or someone else's, whether it's large or small or medium-sized, whether it's for profit or a charitable institution, the bottom line is the bottom line. How do you, the Boomer manager or the ambitious Gen Xer, evoke effective and successful business behavior from your employees when the rules have clearly changed forever?

## Rule One: Use Clear, Straightforward Language

First, any Boomer manager must initiate a new approach that incorporates the viewpoint of the younger generations.

Always say exactly what you want your staff to do. In general, I have found Boomers and Matures—the senior management—are often reluctant to give clear, direct, specific instruction about what they want an employee or subordinate to do; perhaps it seems too blunt and rude to them to give a direct order.

Instead, they speak in generalities or suggest a method, plan, or behavior. For example, every order is couched in phrases such as:

- "You might want to consider . . ."
- "Have you thought about . . ."
- "If you have time you should . . ."

To the dismay of executives, Gen Xers and Millennials hear these suggestions and take them as just that—suggestions. They do not assume that what you say is an order and should be taken literally. For them, the words you spoke are thoughts that came from someone (remember how they see bosses) who may or may not have done the same job himself or herself. So, according to a strict interpretation of what you said, those words are merely options for consideration, not instructions.

However, Boomer and Mature managers are not making suggestions; they really mean "Do it." Gen Xers and New Millennials are caught completely off guard when their managers follow up days, weeks, or months later and expect an account of how their orders were followed and what the results were.

"What did you do about that issue we talked about?"

"You didn't ask me to *do* it," they want to say. "You *suggested* it," or, "You asked me to *consider* it." This creates a problem for the employee, who appears either to have disobeyed the boss or to be too lazy to act on the boss's suggestions.

Generation X and the New Millennials want and need clear, concise, and direct communication. They want to be directed in their jobs. There should be no hidden messages or "They should know what I mean" type of communications. Younger employees have very little tolerance for what they consider to be games played by the older generations. "If you want me to do something, tell me. If you have a clear plan for how I am to proceed, please make it known to me. I'm not interested in trying to figure out some vague suggestion."

Keep in mind that, as a Boomer, you entered a workplace where bosses essentially said: "Welcome. Glad you're here. Good luck. And by the way, we have some rules of the road here that you'll have to figure out. And if you don't figure them out, you'll be replaced immediately by one of the 77 million other job applicants out there. So get in line, keep up, and if you don't hear from us assume you're doing well."

This was the workplace that the Boomers found and that far too many believe still exists.

### The More Things Change . . .

At first glance, you might think that an obvious fix as simple as a slight modification in language would be easy to achieve, and that managing across the generational divide requires only a modest adjustment. I have found several reasons why this is not as easy as it sounds. The first reason is that most people manage others the same way they were managed, and they resist a change in technique.

When training entry-level Gen X and New Millennial employees, Boomers give out the same instructions that they got when they entered the workplace. Why doesn't this work? The difference is that today Gen X and the Millennials don't experience the pressure to perform that the Boomers did. While they certainly are concerned about being fired or replaced, the loss of a job doesn't carry the same stigma it did for the Boomer and Mature generations. It simply happens. Remember, they've watched their Boomer parents suffer, so they are not an overly optimistic bunch. They're not defeatist, either; they simply accept today's workplace as it is. Like the sun and the rain, you will eventually need to change jobs, whether you are fired, are laid off, or can't get along with the boss any longer. This reality is not to be embraced, but it is not to be feared, either.

### Rule Two: Don't Assume Anything

When the Boomers say, "I'm not going to give you all the answers. You'll have to figure them out just like I did," Gen Xers and the New Millennials respond with, "I'm not going to play these silly games. If you want me to do something, tell me. Don't expect me to find the Rosetta Stone to interpret what you really mean."

Communication issues are often at the root of problematic generational differences. Even if you think you have modified the way you tell your employees what is expected of them, even if you believe you are giving a clear, specific instruction, do not assume that Gen Xers and New Millennials see it and understand it the way you do.

Here are some guidelines that work:

- Don't assume they grasp what you're saying. If you're hinting at something or beating around the bush about something, chances are they're unclear about what you mean. They aren't dense; they're simply more accustomed to direct talk. Direct talk need not be harsh; it needs to be clear.
- When you need something done, spell out what you want, when you want it, and how you want it done. This is particularly important for employees coming to work at their first jobs. Develop a routine for giving instruction. It might even be helpful for you—and your employee—to write out the steps required to accomplish a particular task, especially if it's been decades since you did that work yourself. It may seem time consuming, but Gen Xers and New Millennials have never

had to figure out the answers and rules to keep a job. They will, however, learn what to do if they are well instructed, and, since they are technologically savvy people, they will probably figure out a better way to do it.

- You're the boss, so don't be afraid to say, "This is what I need you to do," instead of, "It is important to me that you...." Gen Xers and New Millennials seek work in nonhierarchical environments where the bosses' opinions and suggestions carry no more weight than anyone else's. The phrase, "It is important to me..." doesn't mean much to them. Ask yourself whether it is about the work or your ego as the boss. Don't assume that, because you are the boss, supervisor, or manager, your suggestions will be understood as directions. They won't be.

A Gen Xer working for a hospital in the D.C. area said:

"This is something that I constantly struggle with. My Boomer bosses say, 'It might be a good idea to do X.' I hear a suggestion to do X, which means to me just that—a suggestion. I can take it or leave it, depending on whether I have time or I think it might be helpful to accomplish something in particular. However, the Boomers actually mean, 'Do X.' It's a matter of communication styles. For me it's aggravating to have someone beat around the bush. Don't just suggest things if you definitely want me to do them. Tell me to do them, but let me decide how. Just make clear what you mean in the most precise communication you can."

### Rule Three: When an Employee Gets It Right, Celebrate!

For Matures, celebration in the workplace came only with retirement, the ceremonial close of a career marked by the bestowal of a gold watch plus a handshake from the boss. Boomers celebrated promotions, which were awarded in recognition of years of visible hard work and long hours.

What do Generation Xers and New Millennials celebrate at work? So far, nothing closely related to the job. In most offices today, employees celebrate the birth of a baby, weddings, engagements, and other personal events. But they don't celebrate the key achievements in a person's work life as past generations did. Promotions are appreciated, and bonuses are gratifying, but they are not ballyhooed as they were for the Boomers. It's possible that celebration of promotions and loyalty isn't what work means to these generations. A cynic could also say that these employees are rarely promoted because they don't stay in any one place long enough to be rewarded. But the promotions are coming, especially for Generation X, as they age into and inherit the positions the Boomers leave behind upon their exodus from the workplace and into retirement.

Ask yourself: What behaviors do you want from your Gen X and New Millennial employees? You know they won't be working with you over the long haul—their natures won't allow it. They'll probably change jobs in three to five years. So you'll have them for a limited period of time, and that will give you a unique chance to shape their business behavior.

In all likelihood, they won't come to you ready to work. Those skills will have to be hammered out by their supervisors (and sometimes by their more experienced co-workers). One way to create the behavior you're looking for is to find ways to recognize and reward the desired behaviors in your workforce and then celebrate them. What is celebrated is repeated. Are you looking for timeliness? Excellent customer service? Sales achievements? Pick what you want, a few behaviors at a time. Then, figure a way to measure the achievements so that you and the employees themselves can track their successes.

And remember, these two generations are used to instant feedback and instant gratification. As soon as you get good results, you need to celebrate. Plan in advance and have something ready to acknowledge that behavior.

For example, do you seek customer feedback on your customer service through customer surveys? Is there a way to immediately recognize employees when the surveys come in with positive feedback? Maybe tie a balloon to that person's chair? Turn on a flashing light where everyone can see it? Post the survey on the bulletin board as soon as it comes in?

Do you need your employees to meet strict deadlines? Is there something you can do for them when they meet the deadline early?

---

### Working Hard Card

In some retail businesses, companies have developed a reward for employees who are seen giving superb customer service. Called a Working Hard Card, it is an 8½ × 11 inch sheet of paper cut in half with artwork designed to make it look like currency. When a manager sees an employee giving super service, he/she immediately recognizes the employee, on the spot, with a Working Hard Card. Its value is 30 minutes of time off. Employees are allowed to collect up to four hours' worth of cards (eight cards) and cash them in for time off. There are plenty of rules on how much lead time is necessary to cash them in (usually around 10 days for scheduling purposes), and it must be made very clear that the cards have no monetary value. They've proven to be very effective.

Or in sales environments, if they make the number of sales or sales calls, have something ready to acknowledge that behavior.

What reward to give? While gifts and other perks such as dinners or parties are always welcome, personal recognition from the boss will carry much more weight. This personal outreach is lost in many workplaces today—the boss shaking the employees' hands, looking them in the eyes, and thanking them. Give it a try.

It's easy to say that these simple demonstrations of personal recognition shouldn't be necessary. And many people do say that employees should enter the workforce ready to work and ready to behave properly. But it simply isn't happening. Blaming the parents, the schools, media, or something else won't change the outcome. So deal with it: *You* are the one responsible for creating the reliable workforce of the future. Begin by celebrating the behaviors you want. Think about potty training. You get the idea.

Throughout most of the twentieth century, until the mid-1990s, workplace management functioned effectively with a one-size-fits-all management style: The same rules applied for everyone, no one was special, and no one got special treatment. Employees never expected anything different. And, hey, let's face it—it worked! Look around. We enjoy the spoils amassed by that society. But that model won't work anymore as we move forward in this new century. Individuality has taken root in our society, and today's employees expect to be treated as unique and special individuals. When they've done well, they want to be acknowledged both as teams and as individuals. Parents, schools, and even youth sports have become sensitive to the needs of the individual—everyone is special and everyone is unique. And management today, to be most effective, must function with that as a primary consideration.

# 8

# Creating a Twenty-First-Century Workplace

*Fast, Functional, and Multigenerational*

Age diversity among employees will be a thorny issue for the foreseeable future. No matter what business you're in, you know that to keep your workplace moving forward you need an infusion of youth, fresh ideas, technological skills, and physical energy. But if you're a Baby Boomer, this can come at a great cost of time, energy, and patience. You may even wonder if dealing with these Generation Xers and New Millennials is actually worth the effort. Sometimes you even think you'll be able to get by without hiring additional young people—and then you can just shut your doors when the last of your peer-group employees retire!

Even though you've probably seen *some* motivation, potential, and even exceptional skills in your young employees, this positive behavior is sporadic and unpredictable. You'd like to know how to get consistently high performance from *all* your employees. Perhaps you've already tried everything you can think of, and you need new ideas to refresh your way of thinking.

131

For others the following may be true: You've examined your workforce, realized there is no one climbing the ladder to take over once your generation has retired, and you have no choice but to prepare and train the next generation of workers. Their facial piercings conjure images of falling face-first into a fishing tackle box, and you know they're going to be a challenge. So what can you learn about them before you begin this arduous task?

Here are the four steps you must take to bring your workplace up to speed for the twenty-first century. Take your time thinking over each one before you begin to adapt it to your particular circumstances.

### Step One: Identify the Problem Areas

Ask yourself these questions when thinking about your employees:

- Where am I seeing the problems?
- Where do I expect problems?
- Is there resentment over special treatment of the senior members (including me) in my workplace?
- Do I have a hard time getting my employees to come to work on time or at all?
- Is there a general lack of motivation in job completion?
- Are any employees not treating the customers well?

Then ask yourself:

- Can I determine who on my staff is struggling more than others?
- Is turnover especially bad in one department, in a specific division, or under one specific manager?
- Is there one type of job within the organization that is experiencing more trouble than another?

Next ask:

- Are some of my managers not struggling with this problem, but instead effectively leading employees of all ages?

You might want to consider talking to the successful managers about how they work their staffs and then observing them closely while they work so that you can learn what they do and how they do it. They may be onto something that would be valuable to learn.

## Step Two: Rate Your Success in Hiring the Best Talent

You know the kind of employees you're looking for, whether they are office workers who have mastered high-tech concepts and equipment or skilled industrial laborers. Whatever the position, there is no doubt that talented and dedicated new hires are hard to find today.

However, there are also, without a doubt, a good number of well-trained, tech-oriented Gen Xers in the workplace. Many of them are looking to move on, since changing jobs is the most likely way to secure a raise, even if it's a lateral move. Chances are you're targeting the best and brightest of this group and are fighting lots of competition to win them over. Even in tough economic times, there's stiff competition for talented employees.

There are some manufacturing communities, especially in industrialized nations, that struggle to find competent employees (and in some cases, *any* employees) who want to work in a factory environment. Industrial towns struggle to retain enough young workers to provide the factories with a continuous supply of inexpensive labor.

So ask yourself where you're having hiring challenges. Is there a particular position within the company that is becoming harder and harder to fill? Are there generational factors affecting your hiring processes that you need to consider?

**Step Three: Now That You've Got Them, Learn How to Keep Your Gen X and New Millennial Employees**

The workplace has changed dramatically in several ways, making it even more difficult for Boomer managers to hold on to good workers.

- The Bureau of Labor Statistics reports that the average midtwenties employee leaves his or her job every 1.3 years.
- Kids today are taking longer to grow up than they ever have before. As I mentioned in Chapter 5, more than half of today's college graduates plan to return home to live with their parents instead of striking out on their own with a new job and a cheap apartment. They're marrying later and having children later. They're choosing careers later than previous generations. It is feasible to say that today's youth have been able to extend their adolescence by as much as five to eight years, making decisions at the age of 27 that the Boomers were forced to make in their early twenties. Are Boomers managing employees who are younger than their years? Compared to the Boomers' own experience, absolutely.

The good news is that if you can keep employees on the job for four years, their turnover numbers drop dramatically because it becomes an inconvenience and a burden for them to change jobs. They've finally figured out the politics, they know how they can do their job effectively, and they have ambitions within the company. The bad news, at least so far, is that the odds are against being able to retain Gen X and New Millennial employees for that long.

First, make sure you have clearly defined a younger employee's role in the company. Some Baby Boomers were told to figure it out on the job. They had to learn on their own what their role was in the company; it wasn't given to them. Alternatively, if they were sufficiently competitive, and circumstances favored proactive behavior, they might have invented a new, clearly defined role that proved valuable to the company. The concept of "reinvention" was big in the Baby Boomer lexicon. One boss would tell his employees, "The best jobs are the ones you make." But today, Generation X and New Millennials want to be told where they fit in, what their roles are, and why they're in their jobs. They don't want to figure it out for themselves.

I've used the word *role* deliberately, as opposed to *job description*. A job description is something you give to employees that tells them exactly what is expected of them each day. It outlines the processes and procedures clearly, so there is no misunderstanding.

---

**Job: Front Desk Staff Person at a Hotel**

 *Job Description*

- Greet each guest with enthusiasm and make eye contact.
- Take impressions of guests' credit cards to have on file.
- Direct guests to their rooms using maps provided at the front desk.
- Resolve any billing issues to the satisfaction of both the guest and the hotel.
- Maintain a neat and organized appearance. Your personal dress uniform should be pressed and clean, and the front desk area should be uncluttered and neat.

*(Continued)*

- Answer incoming phone calls by saying, "Good morning/afternoon/evening. Thank you for calling _____. How can I assist you?"

### The Role

Often the first personal contact a guest has at the hotel is with the front desk clerk. This initial interaction is a significant part of determining a guest's overall satisfaction with the stay. It is the proverbial first impression, and therefore it is very important to deliver top-quality customer service to each and every guest.

Additionally, you play a considerable role in the guest's decision about whether to return the next time the guest needs a hotel in this area. For a hotel, repeat business is heavily reliant on guests' interaction with front desk personnel, so a lot is riding on your ability and that of your front desk peers to resolve customers' issues to the satisfaction of both hotel and guests.

You also act as a support system for the engineering and housekeeping department by relaying customer complaints or requests about room upkeep to the correct department immediately. You serve as the guests' first contact on any sort of room upkeep complaint and follow up to make sure the complaint is addressed and solved in the shortest time possible.

In short, your role as a front desk clerk at this hotel is to see to it that guests have the most pleasant stay possible and to use your best judgment to make sure, to the best of your ability, that each guest is accommodated. Your success within this organization will be determined by how you interact with guests, make them feel welcome, solve their problems, and support the other staff members.

A person's *role* in the company is less specific. It is a macro versus a micro designation. *Role* refers to the value of a person's job. It includes how well an employee fits in and works with other departments, and how that person's work factors in with bottom-line priorities, such as sales and fulfillment. A person's role is the reason an employee works for the company, not the particular job.

There are important distinctions between a job description and a role:

- The job description is a step-by-step, play-by-play description of how the job is to be executed.
- The role description offers less detail but gives an overall picture of the value of the job when executed properly.
- The job description details tasks.
- The role description defines responsibilities.

In general, most employees who understand their role in the company attack their tasks with more verve and gusto. It's reassuring for them to understand how their work fits into the bigger picture. As I noted, the Generation Xers and New Millennials want their roles defined for them. A Boomer manager may want young employees to figure this out for themselves, but the young employees want it spelled out in detail.

Why do these new generations of employees want all this hand-holding and attention? It's actually quite simple, if you look at their backgrounds: Xers and New Millennials want to know how they fit into the bigger picture because they don't want to be insignificant cogs in the large impersonal organization.

### Six Things to Remember When Discussing Your Employee's Role

**1.** The role is the macro view of why performing the job description is important to company.

**2.** The role is where the employee fits into the bigger picture.

**3.** When hiring and training your employees, be sure to discuss their roles in the company, which are more important to them than the job description.

**4.** Get your employees' input into what they want their individual roles to be, especially if the job description isn't satisfactory. Work with your employees to develop plans that will help grow them into their targeted roles.

**5.** A person understands his or her role in the company best when it is discussed face-to-face between manager and employee. Do not write out the role as you see it, hand it to the employee, and expect him or her to get it. It is critically important to spend time discussing the role and for you to answer any questions about it.

**6.** If you can't get the employee to accept his or her role, it is best to find a new place for this individual in your company rather than force compliance with the role you've assigned, especially if you believe the employee has potential within the organization.

## Step Four: Spend Time Getting to Know Your People

"If you don't hear from me, assume you're doing well." This management cliché is probably not used as often as you might think because most Boomers know that it's not the reality of a good boss-employee relationship. Underlying this statement is also the idea that bosses and employees don't get to know one another—they don't socialize or become friends. Work is work, and friendships are with other people, not co-workers and certainly not subordinates.

Another oft-repeated management ideal is the open-door policy. The boss claims to allow unfettered access by keeping the door open so that employees can come by and discuss the issues important to them. Once again, this is debatable. I've heard plenty of stories of bosses who claimed to have an open-door policy, but everyone knew that you should never cross the threshold of that office unless you were invited.

Given the choice, Generation Xers and New Millennials prefer an open-door policy to one of noncommunication. But the policy, as it now stands, requires these young employees to take the initiative in communicating with the boss, instead of the reverse. A manager saying "Come to me when you have a problem" is not being proactive and not trying to know his or her employees. Gen Xers and New Millennials are looking for an employer who is interested in them, cares about them, and wants to get to know them. There's a difference between saying "I'm here to listen" and going out and getting to know your people.

When interacting with Gen X or New Millennial employees, broaden the topics of conversation and don't focus on work to the exclusion of everything else. If your goal is to get to know your employees, let them talk about the things that are important to them, which may make you realize that work isn't necessarily high on their lists. As a dedicated Boomer, this might seem foreign to you. However, in the long run it pays off to allow your employees

### The Card Game

 A high-level corporate executive recalled this story from the time when he first became a vice president in an international company while still in his late thirties.

In the 1990s, management socialization was encouraged, and often bosses and assembly-line workers found themselves on the same softball or bowling teams, a decades-old tradition. However, there was also usually another game going on—a fairly serious poker night. Within a few months the young VP was invited to sit in when a regular player couldn't make it. The participants included the CEO, whom just about everyone feared, and several of his peers.

Unfortunately, this VP didn't really play cards. In fact, he wasn't in a position to lose even the $100 minimum stake. However, declining the invitation would be a bad option for several reasons. Even though he played on the softball and golf teams, he feared appearing antisocial. ("Oh, it's just some fun—no work.") He did not want to look stupid or appear to be a failure in front of the boss or his peers. The smart recourse would have been to claim a prior engagement, but the old Baby Boomer "face time" training won out. Needless to say, it was a disaster. He lost double what he could afford. When asked if he would make the same decision again, he still couldn't truly say he would not. This is how deep the Boomers' ingrained training goes.

to lead the conversation so you can learn about their families, hobbies, and lives.

Leadership is very much about telling people what you need from them. But they won't listen to you unless you've listened to them first. You must show them you care and that you are paying attention.

## Be a Leader, Not a Friend

It is always important to remember what Gen Xers and New Millennials are really looking for in a boss: role models, not buddies. It's important for the boss to get to know his or her employees, but don't expect Gen Xers and New Millennials to socialize with their boss after hours, share in company gossip, or become a confidant for inappropriate material.

Today, relationships among employees and managers must remain on a professional, arm's-length basis. Knowing and being interested in your employees is different from becoming their friend. Gen Xers and Millennials typically have plenty of friends, so finding role models, mentors, guides, and leaders at work is sufficient. Too often these younger generations have been disappointed by their parents, who should have served in these roles. The boss needs to be out front, pushing for his or her people to succeed. You should coddle employees only when it is appropriate and kick them in the backsides when things go wrong. This is not the role of a friend; this is the role of a leader.

It may be confusing to a Boomer manager, but Generation Xers and New Millennials don't want to be bossed, and they don't need more friends—they want to be *led*.

## Does Your Character Count?

Does all of this mean that the new generations of workers will simply be mindless, bland automatons, marching to someone else's directions?

No, not even close. Character has always counted, and it always will. Unfortunately, character seems to be harder and harder to find among employers and managers. But do we all have the same definition of character, and what does it mean to the Boomer managers?

There are many different definitions of what character is. The simplest and most effective for managers is: "Do what you say and say what you do." It's very simple. It means being reliable, trustworthy, and always doing the right thing even though it may be uncomfortable to do so.

Generation Xers and the New Millennials gravitate toward bosses with strong character. They test their employers to find out if they have it. When they find it, they stick close to those leaders. As I've said many times in this book, Generation Xers and the New Millennials are loyal to people, not to companies. And it is the people with character who attract the young employees, retain the young employees, and keep them highly productive and hardworking.

Generation Xers and New Millennials are superb studiers of people. They've had a hard time finding character in people most of their lives, but they know it when they see it. Once they do, they loyally follow and trust that person with their careers.

# 9

## Practical Plans, Proactive Approaches

### *The Rubber Hits the Road*

**Don't Dictate—Negotiate**

Some people assume that when Generation X and New Millennial employees come to their bosses to ask for special favors—additional time off, a revised work schedule, pay advances—the employer should grant these requests; not doing so will drive the employees away. If they don't get their way, they'll leave. That is largely untrue.

As a manager, the thing to do is negotiate with your employee. The answer isn't "Yes"; it's "Yes, but what are you going to do for me?" The first time you bargain with an employee, you might think that person will quit. But in fact, she or he is impressed with the negotiation. The difference is that when you grant everything asked for, you're seen as a pushover—and pushovers rarely get any true respect. If, however, you were to blankly say "No," you'd be seen as inflexible—and no one wants to work with an inflexible person. Negotiation is the way to go, and your people will respect you for it.

## The Scale

At a presentation in upstate New York, I was introduced to the idea of the Balance Scale by an audience member. When he hired each of his Generation X and New Millennial employees, he drew the scale for them and explained how it applied to his workplace. The more I've thought about the scale, the more sense it makes, but I've altered it a bit to better reflect the generational dynamics of today's workplace.

Figure 9.1 illustrates what happens when employees demand too much from the workplace for their personal benefit. For instance, individuals want to change schedules to suit their needs, add time to their vacations, and so on. The "Employee" side of the scale is dipping too low—he's heavy because of all the special attention he is demanding. This employee requires too much attention and energy from the company to keep him happy. For the employee, it's a short-term way of acting because it shows that he is not a team player, but

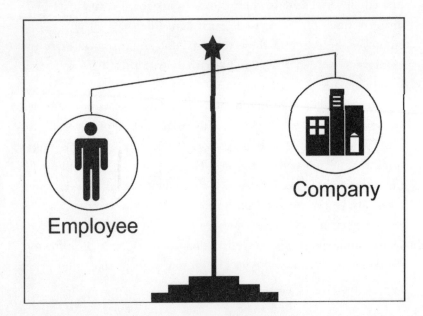

FIGURE 9.1    Balance Scale I

is interested mostly in himself. For an employee to act this way and get away with it, he must have some very valuable and irreplaceable skills that his workplace cannot do without. Otherwise, he's not worth the effort.

Figure 9.2 shows what happens when the company demands too much of its employees. Employees are working too long and too hard. They don't have enough personal time to pursue their outside interests. They're sacrificing too much on behalf of the company. This will drive employees away, and again, it's a short-term way of thinking. In a down economy, companies can force employees to knuckle under because employees need their jobs. But more and more, regardless of the economy, employees are unwilling to sacrifice very much for the company, whatever their age. To Gen Xers and New Millennials, this scenario is untenable, regardless of economic conditions. They value their personal time too much. Remember, they are not their work; their work is what they do to afford who they are.

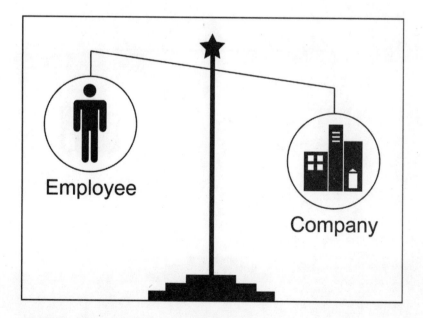

FIGURE 9.2    Balance Scale II

Figure 9.3 is, of course, the balance a company and employees must find to work well together. This can be achieved when a company (1) does not ask too much of its employees and (2) knows what it's willing to give employees *before* they've been given too much. Balance also comes through negotiation when employees ask for specific attention or extra perks or benefits. It is a give-and-take relationship. And each side of the scale may rise or fall as economic conditions change, business success ebbs and flows, and employee demands change. It is not a static situation, and continuous adjustments are necessary to keep the balance in place.

Give some thought to drawing this scale out on paper when you talk with employees. Use it as a visual guide to show them how their needs must be balanced by the company's needs. Let them see that the scale must remain level in order to serve customers, keep the company running, and allow everyone to be happy. It's a very

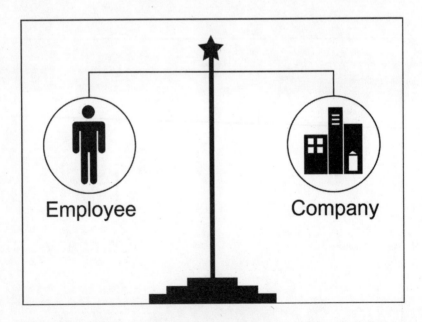

FIGURE 9.3    Balance Scale III

good time to explain that employees become *valuable employees* when they are willing to work with their employer to keep the scale in balance.

Increasingly, young employees today seek a relationship with their boss. Many Boomer bosses interpret this as employees wanting a friendship, which, to the Boomers, is inappropriate in the workplace. My research reveals that what actually is being sought isn't a traditionally defined friendship, but a sincere recognition by the employer that the employee is a unique individual, not just another cog in the machine. Employees want to connect with their bosses, not have orders barked at them. They want to be taught, not commanded. Here is a four-step process for bringing this new type of relationship to fruition.

## Step One: Anticipate the Expectations of the Younger Generations

- Generation Xers and New Millennials aren't looking for bosses who will be their friends. They're looking for bosses who will inspire them in their work and lead them.
- Character is as hard to find today as it has ever been. Young people are searching for it. They'll gravitate toward it. Working for the right person is more important to them than being paid a lot of money.
- The simplest test of character is to ask yourself: Do you do what you say and say what you do? (Or do you play political games with your employees?) Are you dependable in your actions, behaviors, and emotions? Are you reliable? Are you true to your word?
- Granting your employees their every wish is actually detrimental to your operation. When your employees approach you for special needs, don't immediately say "Yes" or "No." Say, "Let's negotiate." You'll gain respect that way.

- Remember and use the Balance Scale. Draw it out and explain how both sides of the scale need to compromise for the scale to balance.

- Managers can no longer manage everyone the same way and still be successful. Each individual in the workplace must be acknowledged as unique.

### Step Two: Develop a Plan for Personal Growth and Development with Each of Your Employees

#### Emphasize Learning

Generation Xers and New Millennials value learning, enjoy learning, and are good at learning, and they like teaching themselves. That's why they have technological skills, which are basically self-taught. They've found that the more they work with a device, the more their skills develop. (Have you ever asked a help-desk person how she fixed something? Often she can't tell you—at least not in a language you can understand.) These young employees believe their value to the workplace consists of what they know and what they can do. This is in direct contrast with the Boomer idea that their value to the workplace derives from their work ethic instead of their knowledge and skills. The differences are important when devising this plan.

To keep your Generation Xers and New Millennials engaged in their jobs and interested in your workplace, it must become a place to fulfill their desire to learn continuously. Whatever their level of education, whether it's high school, college, or graduate school, they know their formal education guarantees them nothing in today's workplace. A college degree today is as common as a high school degree was 50 years ago—nothing special. Gen Xers and New Millennials increase their value by what they can learn on the job that will help them develop in their careers.

### Make a Clear Outline for the Future

Baby Boomers were told by their superiors that if they did their job well they'd eventually be rewarded with a promotion, a raise, and new responsibilities. There was never a time line set for when the new responsibilities would come; a secret system for evaluating employees, hidden deep somewhere in the minds of upper management, would decide. When the reward came, it was a surprise and a time to celebrate.

Gen Xers and New Millennials aren't interested in waiting for the day they are chosen, out of the blue, by management to be told that now is the time for them to move on to bigger things. They're much too impatient and unwilling to commit years to the job in the hope of something bigger in the future. They want to know how they're going to grow their job skills and their careers on a much shorter and more visible time scale. "What is going to happen to me here?" they're asking. "What can I expect to learn, and how will that benefit me?"

As the manager of these generations, you must be able to articulate the skills an employee must have to complete the job well and how possessing those skills will benefit the employee. In other words, you need to be able to say, "In this position you'll learn the following skills, and this is the way those skills will benefit you wherever you go." At each step along the way, each succeeding job must be described in terms of the new skills the employee will learn and what new benefits will follow.

### Clearly Determine Employees' Goals for Themselves

Beyond new skills, it is important to know what employees want to learn on the job. It may be something specific they have thought about or something they see others doing. Asking an employee what she wants to learn is an important step in proving that you're committed to on-the-job education for the people working for you.

The next step is to understand what the employee wants in the long-term future. Ask the questions, "Where do you see yourself five or ten years from now? What do you want to be doing? Where do you want to be?" You may think that asking such questions will provoke your employee to begin thinking about a new job at another company, but in truth you're investing yourself in that person's future and becoming an ally. My experience is that employers who take an active role in helping employees prepare themselves for the future have lower turnover and higher productivity. And remember, yet again, young employees today are more loyal to people than to companies. If you're the person helping prepare them for their future, chances are they won't leave.

### What about Specific Skills?

Always remember to focus on actually helping the employee grow his or her skills. Merely asking the question and not doing anything about it only creates employee cynicism and distrust. Doing something—taking action—is vitally important.

### Putting It Together

- Write down what your employee says in your face-to-face planning meetings, and emphasize his or her participation in making that plan happen.
- List the skills and the goals you and the employee have talked about and, where possible, attach dates for their achievement.
- List the steps necessary for the employee to learn the skills and to execute them flawlessly.
- Commit yourself to pursuing this plan with the employee, and schedule dates when you'll check in with each other on how the plan is working.
- When there are hurdles, work together to overcome them. In other words, be a part of the plan, become vested in it, and stay on course.

The plan may change course at the employee's request, or because the employee tires of the plan. Fine. As the boss, don't be the one who lets the plan fall behind. As jaded and cynical as Generation Xers already are, they'll lump you into the category of "one of them," another one who doesn't do what they say and say what they do. And New Millennials may never say anything if the plan has lapsed because *you've* allowed it to fall by the wayside, but they'll remember. Follow-through on plans for developing your employees' skills is as important as your part in the creation of those plans. Follow-through is an ongoing event!

**Things to Remember When Investing Yourself in the Development of Your Employees**

- The active part you play in your employees' master plans, their futures, is an important element in developing their loyalty to you.

- Generation Xers and New Millennials regard expanding their skill bases, not having a strong work ethic, as the key to creating futures for themselves.

- Generation Xers lose interest in their work at a job or a company when the opportunity to grow and learn is not available.

- After asking your employees, "What do you want to do?" develop a plan for making that future happen. Track the progress of that plan, updating as necessary every six months or so.

- Don't let the plan go stale or abandon it until there is sufficient reason to stop. Sometimes the employee loses interest, and that is fine. But don't you, the boss, drop it without first discussing it with your employee.

### Avoid Top-Down Authoritarian Mandates

Generation Xers and New Millennials (like everyone else) have opinions about what goes on in their workplace. Whether they deserve to have those opinions is not the issue. They believe they deserve input into what is happening around them. They want influence over their environment. Very often Boomers, who have already been in the workplace for some years, have a better perspective on how things work and what should happen. Nevertheless, the younger two generations want to be heard.

Too often, from the Generation X and New Millennial point of view, the boss emerges from his or her office or from some committee meeting with a new rule on how the office will be run—some new overtime rule, some new sick leave rule, a new vacation policy, or simply a new rule on how the coffee cups in the sink are to be washed promptly and kept clean and orderly in the break room. While this particular edict is intended to benefit the office or strengthen the company's position in the marketplace or whatever, the policy is viewed by New Millennials and Generation Xers as a rule being forced on them, and they'll be reluctant to comply, if they comply at all.

Remember, these generations were always included in family decision making by their parents. "What do you want for dinner?" "What do you want to do today?" "What do you want for Christmas?" The list goes on. They've always had input into their environment. And no one has ever told them there is a significant disconnect between home and office. Similarly, there is a disconnect between school and the office. When Gen Xers and New Millennials enter the workplace, they assume their input will be sought by their bosses just the way it was at home and at school.

### Step Three: It Doesn't Hurt to Ask

When younger employees have been asked for their input into office policy, the policy has a far better chance of acceptance in the workplace. The companies that work well with Gen Xers and New Millennials understand that even though many of the younger workers lack the experience to make such decisions, getting their buy-in is important. Such companies have created new forums—simple committees or brief meetings that include younger workers—where the issues are laid out and agreement is reached on the solutions.

The issues can be presented in three ways:

1. *Is a committee structure worth it?* The committee is given the task of revising or reinventing a policy that isn't serving the company well. While the boss knows in advance what should be done, he or she is aware that just dictating the new policy to the staff may engender resistance. So a committee is formed that includes representatives from different departments around the office. The boss then lays out the problem with the current system and asks for a solution. Often the boss will spell out what the solution must include—stay within the budget, maintain staff coverage throughout the weekend, and so on—and leaves the group to achieve the solution. And ironically, more often than not, the solution is the same one the boss had in mind initially. But had it been stated as a demand, there is a chance the staff would have strongly resisted.

2. *Bring the problem to the group.* The boss asks the group, "What do you think we should do about. . . ?" and the group comes up with a decision. This approach is slightly different from the committee structure in that it is less formal and allows for input from everyone around.

3. *Present the problem, then suggest a solution.* Ask the group to alter the solution in small ways to improve it. In this scenario the boss presents both the problem and the solution and then solicits feedback to adjust the solution to make it better fit the needs of the group being affected by whatever change is being made.

## Step Four: Reward Your Managers Who Do Their Jobs Well

How are you rewarding your managers, and what are you rewarding them for? Today there is a greater demand to do more with less. With the economy sputtering back to life, employers are nervous about rehiring all those they had to let go to survive during difficult times. The economy may dive again, and they'll have to go through the misery of conducting the layoffs once more. But while the economy is returning, employers aren't letting up on the output goals for their people. They're still demanding that their people hit their sales numbers, output numbers, quotas, and more. Although a larger staff would make that goal easier to achieve, it isn't an option for many companies. The attitude is, "We're going to do more with less—it will increase our margins and prevent us from dealing with bloated staffs if the economy tanks again. This is the way it is and will be in the future, so get used to it."

It's not exactly a secret that managers are forced to kick things into high gear to meet the demands placed on them by the market and by their superiors. Often a manager's performance is measured solely on widget counts or meeting sales quotas—how many widgets did we get out the door this month, or how many sales did we bring in the door this quarter? No attention is paid to how well they work with and manage their staff—that's simply considered a normal component of their jobs, something they should just do anyway. That may prove shortsighted in the long run. When this is the case, the staff becomes only a labor tool, not a valuable asset that needs attention and grooming to become even more valuable and more productive.

Assume that all of what you've just read is a reflection of common business attitudes. If a manager drives his department well *in spite of* a multigenerational workplace, should some sort of acknowledgement of effective management of the staff become a part of a manager's measurable goals? Here are six ways to decide:

**1.** How many of a manager's staff members move up within the company because they have been well trained and groomed for a new role with more responsibility in the company?

2. How many young staff members are still working for the company after the Bureau of Labor Statistics' average of 1.3 years on the job? And how far beyond that are they going?

3. How many staff members have worked for the same manager for four years or more? If the majority of turnover happens within the first four years, then retaining staff four years or more should be considered a significant victory.

4. Additionally, what authority do your managers have to motivate and reward their staff members in order to get better performance from them?

5. Is there money available to create ad hoc challenges for managers to hit their goals for the day or week? Do managers have the ability to grant half days off or additional paid vacation days for staff members who perform at higher levels?

6. What latitude do your managers have to effectively manage and reward their staff so that they remain motivated and happy in their jobs?

Until businesses begin recognizing that managers should be acknowledged and rewarded for their managing work, the effective development, professional grooming, and retention of key staff will remain secondary in the office, taking a backseat to widget counts and sales numbers.

Keep in mind the following:

- Your managers will begin refining their management skills when you begin measuring those skills and when the success or failure of their management skills impacts their pay.
- Saying that value is placed on retention, professional development, and employee grooming for greater roles in the company sounds good. Taking action along those lines makes those words real.

- Companies have been saying forever, "Our employees are our greatest asset." If that is true, measure the development and retention of those assets just the way you would any other asset, and reward those who excel.

Figure 9.4 is a graphic that reflects the changing attitude of some of the Baby Boomers today. The triangle represents the large numbers of Baby Boomers in today's workplace. They're mostly steadfast employees and work hard, always competing for the limited number of key positions within their organizations—the arrows almost reaching the top of the pyramid. There are only a few of these positions in each company, which narrows opportunities to reach the top.

Generation X is a much smaller group that has opted to take another path. Gen Xers define success differently, represented by the short arrow at the bottom of the pyramid and the arrows pointing left and right. These arrows represent that while Gen Xers do have

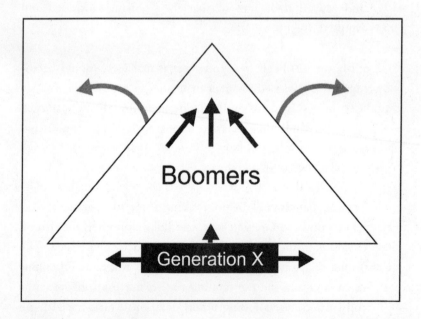

FIGURE 9.4    The Workplace

ambitions to excel at work, they have equal drive for fulfillment out-side the workplace.

The arrows shooting off to the sides of the triangle are Boomers who either (1) have plateaued in their careers or (2) are watching the Gen Xers' and New Millennials' more balanced attitude toward their jobs. These Boomers are asking themselves if it was all worth it—the hard work, long hours, unyielding loyalty. More and more they're an-swering their own question with a resolute "No" and are quietly adopting a Gen X/New Millennial approach to work. The new management ideas introduced in this book will certainly work for Generation Xers and New Millennials, but I'm also finding they're becoming more effective for those Baby Boomers who have reevalu-ated the reasons they work the way they do and have adopted a Gen X/New Millennial attitude.

### Human Resources Is Not Always the Answer

More about hiring: Don't make human resources (HR) your front line when interviewing.

Big companies often send their HR team out to college cam-puses to find their next gaggle of young employees, or HR puts on a hiring fair and someone from the office staff will sit with members of the HR team as they screen each applicant through resume reviews and interviews. While this has been an effective form of hiring for years, companies are unwittingly putting themselves at risk for high turnover when they do make hiring decisions this way.

The element that is missing in this scenario is the critical inter-action between employee and boss. Young people today are very in-terested in meeting and getting to know the person for whom they'll ultimately be working. When HR makes the hiring decision, it's rare for the employee to meet the boss until after he or she has joined the staff. And without giving the employee an opportunity to meet the boss and have a conversation with him or her, this hiring scenario is set up for a high failure rate.

It can't be said too often: Young people today work for the person, not the company. They very much want to meet and interact with the person who will be their boss. And, should they accept the offer to come to work at the company, the new employee knows that, yes, XYZ Company employs them, but it is the boss, the person they have met, for whom they will work. With this distinction in mind, it is foolish to hire a young person today who has not yet had a chance to meet with the boss.

## What to Do Before Making the Final Offer

Beyond meeting the eventual boss, Generation Xers and New Millennials want to talk to their peers about the workplace. They want peer-to-peer testimonials about what it is like to work there. They're somewhat distrustful of the higher-up person who is telling them about the workplace (remember, they want to test authority figures to see if they are who they say they are), and they want to find someone they can trust to give them the truth. The younger the employee, the more they rely on their peers for honest feedback.

Once you've decided that a candidate may meet the criteria you've set for the open position, but before making a job offer, bring the candidate into the office to sit down with the boss and have a conversation. The boss needs to know why this is an important step in the process, so prep him or her about the Generation X and New Millennial biases regarding work and loyalty.

Once the candidate and the boss have finished talking, invite a peer of the candidate into the conversation and allow the two of them to talk about what it is like to work at the company. You, as well as the HR person and others, should leave the room to allow these two young people to talk without your interference and supervision. It's important to brief your employee about why you want a peer-to-peer testimonial in the interview. Encourage your incumbent to be honest and truthful, because the truth will be revealed a short time later anyway. If your new employee realizes he or she has

### Three Things to Keep in Mind during the Hiring Process

**1.** HR should not be the only contact an applicant has with the company before being hired. A job candidate must meet and spend some time with the person for whom he or she will ultimately be working.

**2.** Once a candidate has spoken with her potential boss, encourage her to talk one-on-one with a peer in the workplace. The peer should have had some experience at the company, and her age should be within three to four years of the candidate's.

**3.** Encourage that peer to be candid, honest, and truthful about her work experience at the company. Do not suggest that the peer lie or gloss over the truth, or you'll ultimately lose both the incumbent and the new hire.

been duped and the workplace isn't nearly as wonderful as its description, what you have is a new hire who has been told lies and wants to leave very soon.

The hiring process is too important to be glossed over and hurried through just to get another body into the workplace. In fact, hiring well is one of the most critical elements of a manager's initial success, and an important element in overall management success.

## Administering Reprimands and Giving Criticism

This is a controversial area for many Boomer managers. First, there are simply personal problems—such as, "Hey, take criticism and turn it into a positive." And, of course we live in politically correct times when even a cross-eyed glance can get a manager into trouble. Both Generation Xers and New Millennials are widely known as or at least thought to be sensitive when it comes to receiving a reprimand or criticism. As children they could do no wrong; they were raised by parents who were friends, and rarely were they bawled out.

Today in the workplace, employers have learned that when they

As a volleyball coach of 18-to-22-year-old females, I frequently correct technical skills, but I just as frequently correct behavior. These young women have been coached for years on the way to hit a ball or serve, but I rarely encounter a player who is used to having her behavior corrected. Learning how to receive criticism in the right way has to be trained.

As their coach, I help them learn how to do this so that they can be more productive in the team environment. I coached a player a few years ago who was an incredible athlete and who was a dynamic personality off the court. On the court, however, she tended to pout a lot. If she didn't do something perfectly, she would sulk and would not talk to any of the other players. She never made eye contact with her teammates, and in a team sport these connections are vital. I had many conversations with her in which I explained how important she was to the team and that I wanted to keep her on the court. Her behavior, however, was causing problems with team chemistry and, rather than take her out of the lineup, I wanted her to correct this behavior. Then I detailed the inappropriate behavior and how I thought she could change it. I told her I understood that she didn't have a bad attitude, but that she was just very hard on herself. She had good intentions but poor manifestations of those intentions.

I like to deal with the situation as soon as I can, so that it is fresh in our minds. However, I like to give it enough time so that I can think about what I want to say and give my emotions time to settle. Rarely have I seen a positive result come out of criticism given in the heat of the moment. My players will read my emotions before they hear my words. I definitely tell them how important they are to the program. Then I explain the behavior in unemotional terms. My players can take the tough talks if they understand how they can correct the behavior and that I believe in them.

When I have reprimanded my players in this way and in this sequence, I have found that they are eager to hear about it because then they know specifically how to please the coaching staff. Usually they do not even know they have behaved in this negative manner, so it is eye-opening. They don't want to disappoint me, so they take this conversation as a way to improve their game and their effectiveness within the team environment. On some occasions players have corrected their behavior as a result of the conversation without it seeming to be a reprimand.

criticize their employees for anything or when they need to deliver an admonition, the employee completely loses his or her confidence, performance slows to a sputter, and energy and enthusiasm dwindle almost to the point of shutdown. Sometimes an employee will turn a reprimand or criticism back on the accuser and say that the accuser is actually at fault for not training the employee appropriately. The employee will claim that a lack of leadership, poor mentoring, or inadequate explanation of the rules, not the employee, led to the downfall. All criticism and reprimands are hard for Generation Xers and New Millennials to accept.

There are several effective methods to deliver reprimands that can work quite well. One process is:

1. Talk to the offending individual alone as soon as possible after the incident. Do not have the talk in front of that person's peers or after too much time has elapsed. Do it quickly.

2. Begin the conversation by highlighting the value the employee brings to the organization. Discuss his or her relationships with other employees, services that are provided to the customers, and anything beneficial about this employee in relation to the company.

3. Using neutral language, explain what went wrong and the repercussions. Do not insert your own emotions into the conversation. For example, don't say, "I think you did this because. . . ." Also, do not assume that you understand how the offender feels. For example, "You got angry and did this. . . ." You can never truly know another's emotions. You can make some pretty accurate guesses, but they'll always be just that—guesses. Don't guess; simply explain the behaviors that were witnessed and why they were wrong and what happened as a result.

Now, some employees—especially the younger ones—may be confused. They're aware they're getting a reprimand but it has come in a way that's odd to them: First a compliment (step number 2) and then an account of their offending behavior (step number 3). They've not taken a position on their behavior yet; they've not decided to defend their behavior or admit fault. If you begin calling names, assuming their emotions, or showing an outpouring of your own emotions against the offenders, they'll immediately take a defensive position and you'll be at loggerheads. Making an effective resolution will be difficult to achieve.

4. Together, create a plan to ensure the error doesn't happen again. Make yourself a part of the solution with the offending

party. Make the solution an investment of your time and theirs that will ensure that the same problem doesn't recur.

It's surprising, but when criticisms and reprimands are delivered this way, the offending party is often motivated to produce at higher levels than ever before. The employee may actually have been on the brink of being fired. If the boss did not let that happen and also becomes a part of the solution, the employee sees that the boss has made a personal investment of time and energy to ensure the problem won't happen again. It is a powerful tool.

Preparation is the key to executing this process effectively. Many people find it difficult to do off the cuff. There is nothing wrong with sitting down and planning your strategy before addressing the offending individual. It can't be weeks later, though; it needs to be as soon as possible. But it is better to be prepared than not, because if you falter, the possibility for a good resolution will be lost, and one or both of you will assume a defensive posture. What happens is the boss says, "Do this because I'm the boss and I say so," and the offending party loses steam and complies, but only reluctantly.

Do keep in mind that not all of the age-old management axioms are out the window. These still hold true today:

- In the absence of praise and recognition, people function at a level that keeps them just a step away from punishment.
- People who are scolded and reprimanded change their behavior because they have to. And the behavior change is usually short-lived.
- When praised, people change their thinking and it lasts a lifetime. They might say to themselves, "If they think that was good, they'll be really impressed with what I do when I really try."

Which approach will have a more positive effect on your workplace? You can't praise all the time, but looking for opportunities to praise people and then doing it with sincerity will change their thinking.

## Things to Remember When Giving Reprimands

- Do it when you are alone with your employee.
- Do it as soon as possible after the infringement.
- Refrain from injecting your own emotions or assuming the other party's emotions.

- Develop a plan (that includes yourself) to rectify the problem.
- Prepare in advance to give the reprimand, if necessary.

# 10 | What's Next?

## A Look into the Crystal Ball

A psychiatrist once told me, "The past is the best predictor of the future." I've often wondered if he's right. It always reminded me of another saying that may go along with it, the philosopher George Santayana's remark that "those who cannot remember the past are condemned to repeat it."

What can we predict in the workplace? Will the Boomers fade quietly to retirement communities, as the Matures are doing? Can we foresee that Gen Xers will become more conventional, more like their Boomer bosses? In the next 25 years, will the workplace remain largely the same, with the only real changes being increases in the ubiquity of technology? Will the economy be a more important determinant than age or cultural background in the decisions people make, regardless of their generation, or will generational characteristics and culture play a greater role in people's decision making? And, most important, will Gen Xers who decide to climb the company ladder to leadership learn from the Boomers' own leadership mistakes how to manage—or mismanage—across the generational divide they inevitably will face?

One hopeful possibility is that the generations will take the best from each other. An analogy might be to look at the way each generation has absorbed popular music as a common form of recognition

165

or communication. This may seem trivial, but there is an accurate correspondence. For example, many Boomers still love their parents' music from the 1950s (and 1940s) as well as the rock music they grew up with in the 1960s and 1970s. Many Gen Xers who sat on their parents' laps wearing tie-dyed baby clothes listen to the Beatles and Rolling Stones as much as to their own groups—Pearl Jam, Bon Jovi, and Metallica. It's the same for New Millennials. As frequently as they download Dave Matthews and rap music, they search for the likes of Elton John and other classic rock standards.

### Conservatism on the Rise

There is no doubt that each generation will change in specific ways. I've had a quick look into my crystal ball, and, assuming that the economy and other global problems (e.g., war, terrorism, world health conditions, and numerous unforeseeable events) do not suddenly capsize us, here's my own prediction.

Conservatism is likely to be the general trend and is, in fact, a historical pattern. Every generation becomes more conservative as it grows older. The Boomers are a perfect example. In their youth they were a generation of rebels; now they're controlling the status quo and have recently responded with an uproar over a Janet Jackson performance at the Super Bowl where a so-called wardrobe malfunction revealed the entertainer's breast. Since the incident, the United States Congress, dominated by Boomers, has enacted fines for indecency on the public airwaves that have soared from $25,000 to $250,000. And this from a generation whose constituent members reveled at love-ins and rock festivals that encouraged free love and open sexuality. And, of course, this is the generation whose mantra was sex, drugs, and rock 'n' roll. One of its smash contributions to Broadway was the musical *Hair*, with full frontal nudity.

There is no question at all that Baby Boomers demonstrate a conservative trend linked to aging in many aspects of their lives. Despite their attachment to their music and memories, they play the CDs while cruising in their SUVs and Hummers, or poolside in their backyards, rather than marching in the streets for the environment or to protest the controversial wars in the Middle East.

Certainly, some Boomer values have influenced the workplace and have had a profound impact on social issues (for instance, family leave and equity for women on the job). All of the progress, however, has not exceeded or matched the drive for acquisition—second homes, bigger houses, and an overall affluent lifestyle. Boomers found out quickly that they could achieve these goals only by following the workplace rules laid down by the Matures, who were a very conservative generation. In fact, one of the most interesting signs of Boomers' conservatism is the absence of an outcry over recent governmental intrusions on civil rights that would have sent masses of them into the streets 40 years ago. While the Boomers may have strong feelings about government policies, they don't demonstrate and protest en masse as they once did.

### The Health Care Hustle

Problems with health insurance and the health care system in general are multiplying in the United States. Medical malpractice insurance costs are seriously affecting doctors by driving up their insurance rates to the point where some doctors claim to have quit their practices because they couldn't afford to pay steep insurance premiums. The result is that the best and the brightest of the Boomer generation's income earners have suffered, but only very recently has this sparked any kind of organized reaction over health care issues. Boomers, like Matures, are looking to maintain the status quo and escape into a comfortable retirement.

It's quite possible that one Boomer-influenced organization may end up as a B-school casebook study of the effects of age and wealth on each generation as it matures.

## The Morphing of AARP

The American Association of Retired Persons (now simply AARP) was founded in 1958. Originally, it represented only retirees and supported its lobbying efforts primarily through direct-mail sales of insurance. In fact, it did so much marketing that its building in Washington, D.C., had its own zip code. However, in 1983 AARP realized that with the vast population of Boomers still working, that demographic was where the action was. AARP lowered the membership age to 50. Then, in 2002, they gave their magazine a face-lift. No longer called *Modern Maturity*, it has now been transformed into *AARP—The Magazine*.

Editorially, it morphed into a *People* magazine for Boomers, focusing on celebrities (you are not alone—celebs lose their hair, too); sexuality in late middle age (again, you are not alone—celebs use Viagra, too); and, more recently, social issues (such as the controversial and also very public conservative lobbying in support of the Republican-sponsored Medicare prescription drug reform package). Much of the magazine is aimed at upscale educated and informed people with an interest in social issues, which is probably the reason AARP has recently changed its stance on those reforms. Their readership gave them so much trouble that a recent issue of *AARP—The Magazine* called for allowing Canadian prescription drugs into the United States.

*AARP—The Magazine* also offers the standard club membership benefits such as automobile and hotel rental discounts, but it has focused its advertising sales on companies whose products include pharmaceuticals, safety items for arthritis sufferers, and special diet products for the mature constitution, erectile dysfunction problems, and gastrointestinal stress—all problems encountered in late middle age (again, you are not alone).

In many ways, the growth and evolution of AARP is a signpost for the direction Boomers are taking. It really is not surprising that the generation that once took to the streets to change the world now tends to accept the status quo as a fact of life, and certainly Boomers are more patriotic and supportive of the standard vision of the American dream now than when they were the same age as Gen Xers and New Millennials currently are.

Another indication of the trend toward conservatism is that while the headlines are doomy and gloomy where Medicare and Social Security are concerned, Boomers are still optimistic. A survey by RoperASW for AARP notes some interesting attitudes:

- Baby Boomers are far more likely now than they were five years ago to describe themselves as knowledgeable about and favorably predisposed toward Social Security.
- Boomers are more confident now than they were five years ago that Medicare will be available when they reach age 65.
- Boomers remain optimistic about retirement, but their expectations, particularly those related to finance, have become much more conservative.
- Boomers' primary definition of retirement, however, has remained largely unchanged since 1998: It is an opportunity to spend more time with family, to pursue hobbies and interests, and to enjoy leisure time.

## The Road Ahead for Generation X

If the past is the best predictor of the future, will Generation X inevitably grow more conservative?

One thing I've begun to observe as I work with the oldest members of Gen X is that job-hopping is slowing down. An uncertain economy is one reason, but the single biggest factor is just the one that affected Boomers—Gen Xers are becoming parents. They have kids!

Generation Xers are beginning to understand how smart their parents were in valuing stability. Let's be clear, though—this doesn't mean Gen Xers will simply replicate their parents' behavior, as

Boomers did. That won't happen. Gen Xers will be very different in terms of how they structure their work time and other similar issues, but the need for *security* in their work is becoming more important. Today they ask more questions about health care benefits, retirement plans, and the future of the company. More and more I hear hopes that their employers will remain stable and that they won't have to look for a job anytime soon. Chances are that Generation X workers will change jobs several times more before they stop working. But while their children are still young, Gen Xers seek more stability than they have in the past.

However, I also get a clear message that they won't sacrifice happiness for stability. As I've said frequently, Gen X is in the workplace to "enjoy the ride" as opposed to "living to work" like the Boomers. If Xers determine that the job isn't fun or isn't what they want out of their work experience, they'll think about leaving. But instead of quitting and leaving, which they did when they were younger, they'll stay at their job until they find the next opportunity. This is probably the most significant shift—hanging on to security until something else comes along.

The questions to be answered in the coming decades are whether this employment pattern will pay off and whether the workplace environment has shifted to embrace this sort of work style.

### Time for the Kids

One very important trend now emerging in Generation X is the return of the stay-at-home mom and the three-child household. While the majority of Gen X women work, more and more are opting to stay at home and raise the children, a return to the home/work mix of the storied 1950s. In less than a decade, the number of women staying at home and caring for their children has increased by nearly 13 percent. The number of new mothers returning to work fell by 4 percent. Two-thirds of all working mothers between the ages of 25 and 35, traditionally the career-building years, are working only part-time.

Gen Xers, raised as latchkey kids, have decided they don't really want to raise latchkey kids themselves. And whether they're opting not to work at all outside the home or they're demanding flexible scheduling from their workplace so they can be at home with their children, Gen Xers are determined to raise their children themselves, in person. It is a strong demand and a deliberate reversal of their own childhoods, in which at least one Boomer parent, if not two, spent more time at work than at home.

Employers can also expect that in the future Generation X will continue to put a high priority on control of their own time. This point is scarcely negotiable. Gen Xers have no intention of becoming the workaholics their parents were. It is no secret that time is a sort of currency in today's hectic world, but to Boomers time is less valuable than the money that time spent working can earn. To Generation X, time is a currency with almost the same value as money itself. They'll continue to place as much value on controlling their time as they do on controlling their money.

## Gen X Leaders in the Workplace

As leaders within companies, Generation Xers will do quite well, but their approach toward leadership will differ from that of the Boomers who are in control today. Gen X values completion more than process—just get the job done, on time, and in a quality manner. How it gets done is less important. As innovators they'll continue to create ways for more and more people to become self-sufficient and thereby eliminate the need for groups or teams to complete jobs. Twenty-four-hour offices, home/work stations, cyber-meetings, and other innovations that will develop through improved technology will be common.

Here's the likely future effect of another trend that we haven't considered in depth but that may be significant.

Generation X is marked by diminished workplace-friendly social skills. As latchkey kids with video games, computers, 24/7 television, and divorce, Xers are a generation that interacts inter-personally less and less with their peers and other adults. As a re-sult, those who already have social skills and others who will work to develop them will quickly lead and outshine their peers. They will be celebrated within their companies by their peers and by their customers. They will be thrust forward as leaders whether they want to be or not. They will be very powerful within their generation.

Another challenge on the horizon for Generation X, and a tough one to deal with, is the inevitable day when this much younger generation will be managers of (1) Matures (who have re-turned to work for reasons discussed in Chapter 2), (2) Boomers still in the workforce, and/or (3) Boomers who have also returned to work after trying retirement. Generation Xers will operate and man-age the way they wanted to be managed—that is, merit-based re-wards, more focus on outcome, less focus on process.

Boomers and Matures will struggle with that form of leadership and with their own seniority in years but not in power. This phe-nomenon is already occurring quite frequently, and it will increase in the coming years. Motivated Gen Xers are moving up in their com-panies. Now that they've learned how to succeed, they are leading departments, heading up committees, and overseeing projects. Boomers who report to the Xers are often uncomfortable with these younger bosses, whose basic attitudes differ from the Boomers' about how much time is necessary to complete a job, and where and how to have input on a project.

Many Boomers already bristle at the thought of being managed by an Xer. "How could *they* manage *me?*" But if employees in the fu-ture will be recognized for job completion, not the length of time it takes to do the job and who sees you doing it, then it will be Boomers and Matures who will be forced to understand and ac-knowledge that success is now defined differently.

William Strauss and Neil Howe, in their remarkably insightful 1991 book *Generations: The History of America's Future, 1584 to 2069,* predict that Generation X will become the most conservative generation the United States has seen in a long, long time. In fact, Generation X is predicted to go to an extreme. Their inherent conservatism will increase and take the form of "protect what is mine," whether it is their families, their homes, their retirement savings, their jobs, or their country.

Only time will tell exactly what form their conservatism will take, but undoubtedly the media and technology will have a huge impact on how their conservative behavior and ideals manifest themselves. But if the behavior of Generation Xers as parents is any indicator, creating, supporting, and protecting the family will become much more important. What will all this mean for our idea of work and of the workplace in the future? It will be a supplier to the family, not a dominator of the family.

## New Millennials—A Force for the Future

What about the New Millennials? Will they follow the same predictable future or learn from the mistakes of their Boomer parents? We don't know yet, because so many New Millennials are still adolescents that there aren't sufficient indicators of current adult behavior on which to base predictions.

But, if you consider the great number of profound technological and social changes Matures, Boomers, and Gen Xers have experienced, just try to imagine what's ahead for New Millennials—probably more change in their lifetimes than any of the earlier generations alive today have seen.

New Millennials will be more affected by the changing nature of the economy, which is almost fully global now and becoming more so every day. We know that the nature of work itself will change in the United States. Certainly, we know that our move toward a service economy is already going the way of manufacturing, with more and more outsourcing. New Millennials may have to rely much more on their creativity and ingenuity.

## Hero, Artist, Prophet, and Nomad

In 1997 Strauss and Howe produced a follow-up to *Generations* called *The Fourth Turning: What the Cycles of History Tell Us about America's Next Rendezvous with Destiny*, in which they make predictions for our nation's future based on their studies of generations in the past. They claim that the generations are cyclical and that four generations make a complete cycle. Each generation has existed before; its characteristics, attitudes, and beliefs about society are a repeat of a previous generation. With only one exception, this repetition has existed in the United States for hundreds of years, beginning when we were a British colony. Strauss and Howe assign names for each of these generational archetypes: Hero, Artist, Prophet, and Nomad. Today these archetypes are known as:

- GI Generation (1900–1924)—Hero
- Silent Generation (1925–1945)—Artist
- Baby Boomers (1946–1964)—Prophet
- Generation X (1965–1979)—Nomad

(I refer to the first two generations collectively as the Matures. Since the focus of this book is workplace behavior and the workplace characteristics of these two generations are very similar, they are discussed together here. If I were discussing consumer behavior, it would be necessary to separate them and describe each generation's unique characteristics as they relate to that set of behaviors.)

If these cycles repeat themselves as Strauss and Howe contend, then today's New Millennial generation is another Hero generation. The reliability of this cycle repeating itself can be compared to the stock market—a strong history of performance can be observed, and that history is a good indicator of future performance. But there is no guarantee. Do we know if the New Millennials are another Hero generation? It isn't until adulthood that each generation's characteristics begin to manifest themselves, so we'll have to wait and see, but the odds are that this is another Hero generation.

As Strauss and Howe read history, each Hero generation in the past has had to unite to fight a threat to our society brought on by Prophet generations. Today's Baby Boomers are the Prophets. Whether there will be a fight for the New Millennials to win and what that fight may be are unknowns. Perhaps it is only when the fight is over that we can look back to better understand it. But a few days after the terrorists flew the planes into the World Trade Center buildings on September 11, 2001, President George W. Bush visited the site and climbed to the top of a pile of rubble and with a bullhorn loudspeaker in hand he said to all those who could hear: "We are going to rid this world of terrorism for our children." This may have been the beginning of the fight today's New Millennials will engage in to earn their title as Heroes. Of course we don't know. But those of us who study generational trends and history got chills as we considered whether the cycle had begun again.

Today's Nomad generation is Generation X. In times of battle they are directed by the Prophets (Boomers) and guide the Heroes in the conflicts. After the conflict, the Hero generations then focus their efforts inward and build communities. They provide a posttraumatic healing for the society and create a footing from which future generations will operate. Children born since the year 2000 are predicted to be part of another Artist generation. At this point these children have no agreed-upon name (like Generation X, Baby Boomers, Matures, and New Millennials), but their characteristics, if they are another Artist generation, will be those of caring, open-minded, and sensitive people. On the negative side, though, Artists have been quite indecisive in the past.

Let's return to the New Millennials. Right now it is hard to see them becoming Heroes. But there are signs that New Millennials have a highly developed social consciousness in their concern for the environment and their desire for the inclusion of people of all races and national origins as a matter of course. In their lifetime the phrase *global village* has already become a reality.

## Once Again, Technology Is the Key

Consider: You can instant message with someone on the other side of the globe as easily and as quickly as you can reach the person in the cubicle next to you; there is no time delay—it is truly instant. Today, cell phone technology enables you to answer your calls while you're traveling abroad just as if they were local calls. Video cameras are positioned on buildings in Sydney, Australia, that allow you to watch from your computer as people ascend the Sydney Harbor Bridge on foot.

In the workplace New Millennials will look for guidance and leadership from their bosses for some time to come. While they may have very solid egos, what they often lack is self-confidence. Rejection hurts them far more than it has past generations. After all, they've experienced very little of it. So they'll continue to rely on individuals to guide them until their skins have thickened a bit and they're able to rely on themselves.

Technology will always be second nature to the New Millennials, and they'll be early adopters of the newest gizmos, often to the chagrin of their Boomer bosses, who just wish change would slow down a bit. Peers will be important to New Millennials, and being with those peers—whether in physical proximity or in constant connection via e-mail, text messages, or instant messages—will likely become more important. Unfortunately, they won't see the need to change their behavior in the workplace for a long time, because, as the Bureau of Labor Statistics predicts, their generation will be in huge demand, and jobs will go unfilled as the Boomers retire. When you're in demand, there is little motivation to change your ways.

## Industry Outlooks

There are several industries that will continue to struggle with employee retention, recruiting, and management, based on the behaviors and preferences of Generation X and the New Millennials.

## *Health Care*

Today, health care is one of the service industries that suffers and struggles the most with generational diversity in the workplace. Ironically, it is also the fastest growing and most economically sound sector. Why is there an intergenerational struggle? There are two reasons:

1. Health care traditionally was an industry dominated by women, who until about 25 to 30 years ago had far fewer options for careers than they do today. Teaching, health care, and secretarial work were the easiest fields for them to enter. Today the options for women are limitless, and fewer of them are choosing to enter health care.

2. The massive Boomer population is overcrowding hospitals again, just the way they did when so many of them were born within a short time span. But now Boomers are aging, they require more specialized care, and their demands for care will only increase as they continue to age. More than ever, health care facilities need well-trained staff.

Generation Xers and New Millennials are finding the demands of working in health care a challenge to their lifestyles. They can do the job; that's not the problem, but the time requirements are tough to deal with. As a matter of course, health care is a field in which new hires are given the worst shifts, the most difficult patients, and the oldest technology to work with. To get the best shifts, with the best patients and the best technology, the new practitioners must pay their dues and earn their stripes.

In health care, seniority gets deference. And that's why Generation Xers and New Millennials are opting for work in other fields rather than work at the bottom of such a rigid top-down structure. In an odd contradiction, this generation is desperately needed, but when they enter the workplace they're treated poorly. And in today's employment environment, they don't have to take that kind of treatment—there are too many other options.

Technology continues to radically advance treatments in the medical field, and what generations are more capable of learning and using that technology than Generation X and New Millennials? The manufacturers of this technology can dumb it down only so far in an effort to get it to the point that a Boomer can work it properly. Before too long, the youngest employees will be in much greater demand than they are today because they're needed to do the job, and they're the only ones who know how to work the technology.

Scheduling is the biggest problem the younger generations have working in health care. The scheduling demands of the jobs interfere with Xers' and New Millennials' lifestyles. Health care providers that succeed in recruiting and retaining employees are coming to realize that, with the younger generations, they must negotiate scheduling. The days of working the worst shift because you're low person on the totem pole are over. The days of telling employees "It is time that we renegotiate your scheduling" are in. Consider time as equivalent to currency; like money, it must be negotiated.

## Manufacturing

Right or wrong, jobs in manufacturing often are not considered sexy. Recruiting for manufacturing jobs will continue to be a struggle. These difficulties are compounded because the communities where manufacturing traditionally drove the economy (the Midwest, the industrial Northeast, Appalachia) are now communities that the young people are leaving for what they consider "better places to live."

Gone are the days when people moved to the cities where they could find work, and in are the "hip, cool, and happening" cities to which people move because of the lifestyle qualities (Charlotte, Asheville, Atlanta, Austin, Chicago, Denver, San Diego, Portland, and others). Then they try to find a job.

These problems are compounded by the instability of manufacturing jobs in a post–NAFTA world, with the constant threat of your job being moved overseas and performed by someone working at less than half your salary, receiving no benefits, and having no idea what a retirement plan is or why he or she should want one.

Factory work has been stereotyped: long hours, dirty conditions, and poorly educated co-workers. Today, the technology involved in manufacturing has changed the reality, but the stereotype is still hard to shake. Those challenged with attracting employees to manufacturing jobs will need to work extra hard to get the attention of Generation Xers and New Millennials. They'll need to focus their pitch on what employees will learn on the job and whom they'll work with and learn from. And they'll need to promise and then prove to employees that the job they'll be hired for will be a complement to their lifestyle, not a threat to it.

Given these circumstances and the lure of cheap, compliant foreign labor, it is likely that more and more manufacturing jobs will be outsourced.

### Technology

It is a peculiarity of our times that no single element of business is more integral to success than the one that senior members of the workplace cannot work and cannot fix, nor can they grasp the theoretical background principles that ground it. That element is technology. In the past, senior members of the workplace learned the entire scope of a job from years of doing it, often starting in the proverbial mail room and working themselves up the ladder. This is especially true of manufacturing and retail businesses.

Today, though, if the server goes down, the e-mail backs up, a virus strikes, or the DSL fails, how often do you see a 50-year-old diagnosing the problem on his hands and knees from behind the server and proclaiming to the office, "We need to reboot the server!" Almost never. The notion of an apprenticeship in the technology arena is a 40-year-old working three years for a 22-year-old. It is flipped on its head, completely backwards. And our reliance on technology is not waning; it is increasing dramatically.

Still, the technology frontier is just that—a frontier. What is out there is unknown. Advances are occurring more and more quickly. No industry in the past five years has remained significantly untouched by technology. Businesses will continue to need savvy staff to help them navigate the technology, and those businesses will continue to pay their young experts well because they are scarce. It is the rare field where a tattooed, pierced, orange-haired kid cannot hold his conservative-suited Boomer or Mature boss in the palm of his hand because this kid is the only one who knows what is going on inside the server. What does that mean? It means good pay and a pretty solid future.

Technology is a field that, if I were to do it all over again, I'd take a hard look at.

### Other Service Areas

Some service industries will offer continuing opportunities for young Gen X and New Millennial employees. Primarily, these opportunities will be in businesses where the demand is for customer service and social skills. Such skills, as discussed earlier, are typically taught at home, but for some reason they aren't being taught as well today. People who master these skills, who learn how to treat customers and communicate effectively with them, will quickly rise to the top. Those who don't get it will end up staying in back-room operations and not interfacing with the customer.

People with sales skills will become more important and harder to find. Many employers have expressed their disappointment when, upon hiring a Gen Xer or a New Millennial, they learn that these two generations are extremely fearful of rejection and, after being told "no" by several customers, leave their jobs (or quit trying and stay, which is worse than leaving). Sales managers tell their employees that to be successful in sales one must develop a thick skin, but few of today's youth have that attribute. Why is that? Possibly because of the total acceptance they experienced growing up at home and in school. So instead of redoubling efforts to make sure they don't lose again, these younger employees fold their cards and walk away. Effective salespeople will always be in demand. New Millennials and Generation Xers who persevere through the hardships of rejection, which are inevitable in sales, will find success by sticking to it where their peers choose to quit.

All of these insights into the future are, of course, predictions, not facts, and time will prove them true or false. Earlier in this chapter, I discussed a published study of the generations in history that held that each generation is repeated every four generations. So, using history as a guide, we *should* be able to predict what will come. The stock market is a good analogy: It typically grows year after year. There is nothing that guarantees that it will grow, but it usually does. In fact, it has grown so regularly throughout its history that we rely on its growth and invest money for our futures in it via individual retirement accounts (IRAs), self-employed pension (SEP) plans, 401(k)s, and, more recently, the new health savings accounts (HSAs). But, again, nothing guarantees its growth. Similarly, we can predict some of the particular behaviors, attitudes, and value systems in each future generation that will make individuals in that generation more valuable compared to their peers, but we have no guarantees these predictions will come true.

# 11

## "And Now, a Few Words to My Peers"

### *What Gen Xers and the New Millennials Should Be Told at Graduation*

One of the common events in the lives of Gen Xers and New Millennials is that virtually all of us sat through a commencement speech that almost invariably began: "Today, my friends, we are at a crossroads in our history. . . ."

This was followed by what seemed like several hours of gratuitous advice that had about as much relevance to our lives and futures as many of the required courses we had to take to get a degree that may have cost $130,000 and was of little help in finding a job.

If I'd ever had the opportunity to address my peers at such an event, I would have said something different from what most commencement speakers say. I'd do my best to prepare my generational peers for today's workplace. It would go something like this.

Okay, here it is. As a Gen Xer myself, I don't come from the point of view of a sage, a futurist, or a crystal-ball gazer. For the past decade I've been a salesman and a call-center customer service rep, a customer service trainer, and a professional speaker. Therefore, the following is based on what employers have told me; what you, my peers, have told me; and where the trends in the generations seem to be going.

Here's the first stark reality: Boomers are running the show right now virtually everywhere. They're in control. The vast majority of our elected officials are Baby Boomers, and the bosses and managers in most workplaces are Baby Boomers. They'll continue to promote one another and elect one another for a good while. And, as I've been seeing, when they retire, their peers will go to them and beg them to come back into the workplace when there is a workplace shortage, because Boomers find other Boomers easier to work with.

To be blunt, Boomers will prefer themselves to you and me as long as they can get away with it. They have a distaste for Generation X, and they don't understand their own children, the New Millennials. They love their children beyond all measure, but they don't understand them. Boomers hope their children will get jobs and be successful, but they don't want their kids to work for them.

If that's the landscape right now and for some time in the foreseeable future, what can we do about it?

The first thing we've got to understand and admit to ourselves is that we will have to play the Boomers' game for some time to come. We're like Prince Charles—we'll be in positions of influence but wondering when we are ever going to get to ascend the throne. What does that mean for us?

- It means that we'll continue to be measured against Boomer standards, regardless of whether we agree with that rating system.
- It means hard work will still be measured by the number of hours we spend on the job and who sees us there each week rather than how much we get done in that time.
- It means that we must appear to put the job first and foremost in our lives.

- It means that they expect us to want to be promoted further up in the organization, and they expect that we would rather be rewarded for hard work by money than by anything else.

Does this mean forever?

Thankfully, no. Slowly the Boomers are understanding that their way of doing things is not the only one out there, and that other ways are available to measure success—but it isn't happening quickly. Some Boomers who are still on the job will never believe that what they've done, what they've worked hard for, isn't a valuable path for you and me to follow.

But be clear that I do not recommend capitulation. We'll just have to keep pressing forward without compromising our generation's values. We don't have to bend to the pressures of what they think is right, wrong, good, or bad. We won't let the job consume us, and we won't let the pursuit of success mean ending up at retirement being successful to the exclusion of all else.

History has shown us, and current times continue to prove, that banking on all the work you've done in your life to pay off in the end with a retirement, pension, bonus, or whatever is a pipe dream. It is important to enjoy the ride, enjoy the path, and enjoy the process, too.

How many people have you seen retire and then lose their identity? If they can't go into work and do what they've always done, they don't know what to do or where to go. They get to retirement and realize they have no hobbies. They have no idea who they are without their jobs. Our work is important, but it is not our entire definition of self. Don't let it happen.

We also have some challenges of our own. Both my Gen X peers and the New Millennials (who will overtake us in numbers very shortly) have a few things to learn from those who have come before us.

Our two generations have lived in times of relative wealth. True, we've had our disasters and recessions, and, as a nation, have been quite vulnerable from time to time, but we have not experienced anything close to World War II or the Great Depression. We've not even experienced a Korean conflict or Vietnam War. As of this writing, the conflict in Iraq involves 138,000 American military men and women. That is only 0.0004 percent of our population of 295 million compared to the more than 16 million soldiers in World War II, which was about 11.5 percent of the population in 1945. We've not lived in times of exclusive peace and prosperity, but we don't have many of the extreme experiences of those who have come before us. And while there is no better teacher than experience, we need to figure a way to learn from *their* experiences. It will help us as we continue into adulthood and it will help us in our careers.

### What I've Learned from the Boomers

So here are a few of the kernels of wisdom from the Boomers that I've picked up over the past several years and incorporated into my work style.

First, work to completion—finish the job. Don't just do your segment, your piece, or your assigned parts, but ensure that the entire assignment is complete—take responsibility. In addition, be sure to:

- Complete the job with quality. Quality is not someone else's job; it is everyone's job. That is an old, trite saying, but it is true.
- Learn the scope of your work, commit to working on it until completion, and finish it with quality. It's very important to remember that quality is your boss's measurement, not yours. What does the boss believe is quality work? Get clear on that definition and adhere to it. We don't have to duplicate Boomers' work ethic, but we can learn from their ability to produce quality work.

Second, if you're in sales, search for "no's." A man much smarter than I am once told me that in his sales efforts he sought out 10 rejections from prospective clients every day. And in seeking these rejections he invariably made three or four sales. Rejection was what he sought, not avoidance. Understand that rejection is a part of every job and is critical to your success. It is about being brave. The sooner you can grasp this and accept it as part of what you do, the sooner you'll find success. Remember:

- If you search for "no's" and embrace them, you'll watch your peers fall behind.
- The Boomers and Matures understand that rejection is a part of their job. We need to learn this, too.

Third, learn to talk to people. Learn to look them in the eye and listen. Learn to be interested and learn to be interesting. It is hard to do, but it will pay off. Understand:

- We've been brought up with the Internet, instant messaging, text messaging, and on and on. Too many of us speak and write in a shorthand that is unintelligible to many older adults.
- For us to communicate with Boomers, we must learn the art of conversation. Talking to someone directly is the best way to build a relationship. And while advances in technology will continue to remove us from face-to-face communications, those rarer occasions where we do talk to someone face-to-face will become much more important. They'll be do-or-die moments in establishing relationships based on genuine communication.
- Prepare, practice, and be ready. Baby Boomers and Matures assume they will be able to communicate well. For them, finding Gen Xers and New Millennials who do it well is an exception. We need to learn how they do it.
- If you really want to leap ahead in your business, learn how to make presentations effectively. Learn to get your message across to an audience clearly, reasonably, and forcefully, but

without aggression. Presentation is a skill you can work on and develop. It is a skill that will boost your self-confidence, and it will serve you well with employers and audiences alike.

Learn the value of flexibility in all you do. Our generations have approached the workplace demanding flexible work schedules. What we've neglected is working with our bosses when they need flexibility from us. Until recently we, the younger generations, have been able to make some outrageous demands in the workplace and get away with them. In the future we'll need to be able to accept flexibility when it is asked of us. Flexible employees become valuable employees. And there is a difference between working for a company and being valuable to a company. When you have a job, you simply fill a space. When you're valuable, you fill a need. I encourage you to become valuable. That means learning to talk to people; learning to accept (and maybe even seek) rejection in sales; learning that quality is your job, and your boss's definition of quality is the only one that matters; and becoming flexible in all you do—most important, being flexible with your employer. Don't compromise who you are, but adjust for your job when it's required of you.

Employers look for workers who have a proven track record of focus, discipline, and execution. When they find employees with these attributes they'll fight to hire them and then fight to keep them. Many employees have these talents but lack the characteristics I've just enumerated. I hope you give them some thought and, ultimately, embrace them.

One last thought is simply this: Work for today but plan for tomorrow. What does that mean?

It means enjoy the ride. Enjoy the work. Don't work at something you don't like. Don't work at something that you hope will pay off in the end unless there is an absolutely guaranteed big pot of gold at the end. And be especially careful about being promised something in the future that may or may not come true.

I wish I could count the number of people who told me their bosses promised them a car allowance in a few years, a raise next year, a vested retirement plan after a certain number of years, a one-time bonus for a good job—and have not followed through. Bosses always (perhaps genuinely) want to bestow these well-deserved rewards, but, for whatever reason, they seem unable to fulfill their commitments.

*Don't let this happen to you.* Our world today changes instantly. Money that was once set aside for bonuses may now be needed just to make payroll. The company owner who promises he won't sell his company to the national chain is driving a Mercedes to his new beach house six months later, both bought with profits from the sale he promised his staff he'd never make. It happens all the time. When evaluating your job, look at it on a short time horizon, two or three years at the most. In those three years, things will have changed dramatically anyway, so don't be swayed by what your employer promises might happen in five years. If it isn't on the horizon, don't fall for it.

## Live for Today, But Prepare for Tomorrow

Be prepared for the future. Save and invest wisely. Social Security will be ravaged by the time we're eligible to claim it, which, at this rate, may be age 75, if we're lucky. And if there is something there for us, it will be a mere pittance for us to divide among ourselves. We'll never get back nearly as much as we've paid into it. It is the "cost of doing business" for living in the United States. And frankly, it stinks, but until the Boomers in Washington come to grips with real problems like these, we're stuck with it. So it is our job to prepare for our own futures. Don't ignore this responsibility, or it will completely ambush you. I'm seeing it happen to my older Gen X friends. They're already realizing they're not nearly as prepared to live as comfortably as they'd hoped because they've been spending everything they've earned. Be careful and invest in your future.

Tomorrow you'll all cross the thresholds of your offices, and you'll look your bosses in the eye and prepare for a new day. I encourage you to keep the advice I've just given you tucked away somewhere in your mind and be prepared to call on it when you need to. Chances are your bosses are working hard to figure you out. They need to know how to keep you on the job and keep you happy. But you have a responsibility in this relationship, too.

Do what you can to contribute. Learn everything you can. And live for today, but prepare for tomorrow.

Thanks. Now let's get going.

# Quiz: Generational Voices

## *Who Am I?*

*Select the generation you think the person making each statement would most likely represent. (See Figures Q.1 to Q.4.) Be careful—some of these are tricky.*

**1.** Some people estimate that there were nearly 500,000 of us at Woodstock. But if you survey the country today, you'd have to think the number was more like several million.

    **a. Mature**        **b. Boomer**        **c. Xer**        **d. Millennial**

**2.** My sister's son contracted polio. Fortunately, when my daughter was born a few years later, the vaccine had just come out.

    **a. Mature**        **b. Boomer**        **c. Xer**        **d. Millennial**

**3.** John F. Kennedy was assassinated when I was in junior high. By the time I graduated from high school, Martin Luther King Jr. and Robert Kennedy had also been killed.

    **a. Mature**        **b. Boomer**        **c. Xer**        **d. Millennial**

**4.** Crowded? I can tell you about crowded. The Catholic schools in my neighborhood sometimes had 60 in a class! It made everything very competitive. The good thing was you had to learn how to get along, how to team up with other people.

a. Mature        b. Boomer        c. Xer        d. Millennial

**5.** I think there's a good reason you don't hear much "Oh, he's my hero" talk these days. I just don't think there are many heroes. There are people who are rich, famous, whatever, but not too many heroes.

a. Mature        b. Boomer        c. Xer        d. Millennial

FIGURE Q.1    Matures, Born between 1909 and 1945

**6.** You might not believe this, but sometimes I borrow my mother's CDs. I mean, we don't have exactly the same tastes in music—but we like *some* of the same stuff.

   a. Mature        b. Boomer        c. Xer        d. Millennial

**7.** The year I turned 15, the unemployment rate was nearly 25 percent.

   a. Mature        b. Boomer        c. Xer        d. Millennial

**8.** When I was a junior in high school, the Grammy for Album of the Year went to Bob Dylan for *Time Out of Mind*.

   a. Mature        b. Boomer        c. Xer        d. Millennial

**9.** You might hear "ludicrous" and think: ridiculous. I hear it and want to turn up the radio.

   a. Mature        b. Boomer        c. Xer        d. Millennial

**10.** Once in a while in elementary school, we did these silly drills where we got down on our knees and tucked our heads down with our hands on the back of our heads. That was supposed to help protect us against The Bomb.

   a. Mature        b. Boomer        c. Xer        d. Millennial

**11.** I was just old enough to learn how to drive when I heard about the Chernobyl accident in the Soviet Union. I don't think I quite understood the magnitude of that at the time. I do now.

   a. Mature        b. Boomer        c. Xer        d. Millennial

**12.** Three Mile Island—you don't hear about that much anymore. That was pretty close to the Big Bang revisited. I was just out of college and starting a career. I'm lucky it wasn't a short one.

   a. Mature        b. Boomer        c. Xer        d. Millennial

FIGURE Q.2 Boomers, Born between 1946 and 1964

**13.** Sometimes I get tired of hearing the word loyalty. I think people who have a lot of power like to throw that word down on the people who don't. Look at the record. Look at all the people who were supposed to have long careers and big pensions—and got unemployment and Social Security instead.

a. Mature    b. Boomer    c. Xer    d. Millennial

**14.** You pay your dues. You make the sacrifices necessary to make things work. People today ask too many questions. They expect too much too soon. Just do what you're told. Get the job done. You'll get what you deserve in time. Your company puts a roof over your head and food on your table. You have an obligation.

a. Mature    b. Boomer    c. Xer    d. Millennial

FIGURE Q.3    Generation Xers, Born between 1965 and 1979

**15.** It was the bicentennial year. Everyone was in love with Colorado and looking for a Rocky Mountain high. So we packed up the dog in the van and took off cross-country with no particular route—and hardly a dollar to our name.

   a. Mature        b. Boomer        c. Xer        d. Millennial

**16.** On my first date we went to see a brand-new movie called *Gone with the Wind*. It was pretty good but, my gosh, it was almost four hours long. I was late getting home and my parents were furious.

   a. Mature        b. Boomer        c. Xer        d. Millennial

**17.** Everybody talks about TV this and TV that; this show, that show. I don't really need it that much. There are plenty of other things to do.

    a. Mature        b. Boomer        c. Xer        d. Millennial

**18.** Morning routine: the newspaper and a cup of coffee. It's still hard to beat the newspaper for getting information about things, and a cup of coffee works for me any time of day.

    a. Mature        b. Boomer        c. Xer        d. Millennial

FIGURE Q.4   New Millennials, Born between 1980 and 2000

**19.** I was in high school when *Dallas* was huge on TV. The "Who shot J.R.?" thing was everywhere. Pretty crazy.

a. Mature        b. Boomer        c. Xer        d. Millennial

**20.** When I was a freshman in college, planning to major in political science, the Berlin Wall came down. I was in heaven!

a. Mature        b. Boomer        c. Xer        d. Millennial

**21.** Geraldine Ferraro became Walter Mondale's running mate in a presidential election. I was only 17 at the time. I told my mother I was going to either own my own business or hold public office. She just grinned at me.

a. Mature        b. Boomer        c. Xer        d. Millennial

**22.** When I was a kid the Battle of the Bulge was not a book about getting rid of the spare tire around your middle.

a. Mature        b. Boomer        c. Xer        d. Millennial

**23.** I'll never forget it. I was home from school in the summer. I sat with my mom and dad and watched as tears came to Walter Cronkite's eyes as he reported Neil Armstrong walking on the moon.

a. Mature        b. Boomer        c. Xer        d. Millennial

**24.** I was the only kid in the apartment building to have two Cabbage Patch Kids.

a. Mature        b. Boomer        c. Xer        d. Millennial

**25.** Some members of our generation were to be referred to as "yuppies," supposedly derived from "young, upwardly mobile professionals" or "young urban professionals." Whatever. I don't think it was generally meant as a compliment.

a. Mature          b. Boomer          c. Xer          d. Millennial

# Answer Key: Generational Voices Quiz

## *Who Am I?*

**1.** Some people estimate that there were nearly 500,000 of us at Woodstock. But if you survey the country today, you'd have to think the number was more like several million.

**Boomer.** The Woodstock music festival took place between August 15 and 17, 1969. It was a huge, era-defining event. Today you can ask most Boomers living east of the Mississippi and they will tell you they think they remember being there.

**2.** My sister's son contracted polio. Fortunately, when my daughter was born a few years later, the vaccine had just come out.

**Mature.** The polio vaccine was developed by Jonas Salk, MD, and came into use in 1954. Before a vaccine was introduced, more than 20,000 cases of the disease were reported annually in the United States, and about 1,000 people died each year when the muscles that controlled their breathing were paralyzed.

**3.** John F. Kennedy was assassinated when I was in junior high. By the time I graduated from high school, Martin Luther King Jr. and Robert Kennedy had also been killed.

Boomer. President John F. Kennedy was assassinated in Dallas, Texas, on November 22, 1963. Both Robert Kennedy and Martin Luther King Jr. were assassinated in 1968.

**4.** Crowded? I can tell you about crowded. The Catholic schools in my neighborhood sometimes had 60 in a class! It made everything very competitive. The good thing was you had to learn how to get along, how to team up with other people.

Boomer. The population swell of the 1950s and 1960s overwhelmed school systems and colleges.

**5.** I think there's a good reason you don't hear much "Oh, he's my hero" talk these days. I just don't think there are many heroes. There are people who are rich, famous, whatever, but not too many heroes.

Xer. As a generation, Xers tend to be more skeptical and cynical. When surveyed, many state they have no heroes as a generation. They are the only generation with that response.

**6.** You might not believe this, but sometimes I borrow my mother's CDs. I mean, we don't have exactly the same tastes in music—but we like *some* of the same stuff.

Millennial. This is an example of "parent as friend" and other changes in generational relationships. The traditional cultural schisms between generations do not always hold true anymore.

**7.** The year I turned 15, the unemployment rate was nearly 25 percent.

**Mature. Incredible double-digit unemployment marked the Great Depression of the 1930s.**

**8.** When I was a junior in high school, the Grammy for Album of the Year went to Bob Dylan for *Time Out of Mind*.

**Millennial. A folk icon of the 1960s, Dylan still turns out best sellers and Grammy winners. *Time Out of Mind* won the 1997 Grammy for Album of the Year.**

**9.** You might hear "ludicrous" and think: ridiculous. I hear it and want to turn up the radio.

**Millennial. Music makers I, Ludicrous (rock) and Ludacris (rap) have both been successful.**

**10.** Once in a while in elementary school, we did these silly drills where we got down on our knees and tucked our heads down with our hands on the back of our heads. That was supposed to help protect us against The Bomb.

**Boomer. Did anyone really think that was going to work?**

**11.** I was just old enough to learn how to drive when I heard about the Chernobyl accident in the Soviet Union. I don't think I quite understood the magnitude of that at the time. I do now.

**Xer. In 1986 the Chernobyl nuclear accident in the Ukraine was the result of a flawed reactor design and inadequately trained personnel. Some 31 people were killed, and there have since been 11 deaths from thyroid cancer and hundreds more seriously ill reportedly due to the accident.**

**12.** Three Mile Island—you don't hear about that much anymore. That was pretty close to the Big Bang revisited. I was just out of college and starting a career. I'm lucky it wasn't a short one.

Boomer. In 1979, a malfunction at the Three Mile Island Nuclear Generating Station, near Harrisburg, Pennsylvania, led to the most serious commercial nuclear accident in U.S. history. The system was about 30 minutes away from an irreversible meltdown. More than 90 percent of the reactor core was damaged; 52 percent had melted down.

**13.** Sometimes I get tired of hearing the word loyalty. I think people who have a lot of power like to throw that word down on the people who don't. Look at the record. Look at all the people who were supposed to have long careers and big pensions—and got unemployment and Social Security instead.

Xer. Xers grew up witnessing many of the disappointments experienced by the Matures in terms of lost jobs and evaporated pensions. As a result, many are not very receptive to appeals for loyalty to employers.

**14.** You pay your dues. You make the sacrifices necessary to make things work. People today ask too many questions. They expect too much too soon. Just do what you're told. Get the job done. You'll get what you deserve in time. Your company puts a roof over your head and food on your table. You have an obligation.

Mature. *Loyalty* and *duty* are hallmark words for this generation. They put faith in staying the course and exercising patience in the face of adversity.

**15.** It was the bicentennial year. Everyone was in love with Colorado and looking for a Rocky Mountain high. So we packed up the dog in the van and took off cross-country with no particular route—and hardly a dollar to our name.

**Boomer. The year was 1976. Lots of people used the bicentennial as a time to explore the country—sometimes hitchhiking or in vans and VW Microbuses.**

**16.** On my first date we went to see a brand-new movie called *Gone with the Wind*. It was pretty good but, my gosh, it was almost four hours long. I was late getting home and my parents were furious.

**Mature. Released in 1939, *Gone with the Wind* is still with us. Rhett Butler and Scarlett O'Hara are cultural icons. Its tagline, "The most magnificent picture ever!," continues to find supporters more than 65 years after its release.**

**17.** Everybody talks about TV this and TV that; this show, that show. I don't really need it that much. There are plenty of other things to do.

**Millennial, maybe Mature. Millennials are much more eclectic and are just as happy with video games, computers, and other active pursuits. They are not as devoted to TV as Xers and Boomers are. Matures did not grow up using TV as a primary source of information and entertainment. They, too, often find it easier to ignore the tube and do other things.**

**18.** Morning routine: the newspaper and a cup of coffee. It's still hard to beat the newspaper for getting information about things, and a cup of coffee works for me any time of day.

**Mature. For the Mature generation the newspaper has always been a primary source of information. Coffee, the drink of choice in their formative years, remains a favorite, often consumed at breakfast, lunch, and dinner.**

**19.** I was in high school when Dallas was huge on TV. The "Who shot J.R.?" thing was everywhere. Pretty crazy.

Xer. For millions of people around the world, one of the most riveting events of the times was the March 21, 1980, shooting of Texas oil baron and bad guy J.R. Ewing on the hugely popular TV series *Dallas*. "Who shot J.R.?" was one of the best-kept media secrets ever. Of course, now the answer's common knowledge.

**20.** When I was a freshman in college, planning to major in political science, the Berlin Wall came down. I was in heaven!

Xer. On November 9, 1989, the border separating West Germany and East Germany was opened and the famous Berlin Wall figuratively and literally crumbled. The Berlin Wall was built in 1961 and not only separated the residents of the city, but also became a prominent worldwide symbol of the Cold War.

**21.** Geraldine Ferraro became Walter Mondale's running mate in a presidential election. I was only 17 at the time. I told my mother I was going to either own my own business or hold public office. She just grinned at me.

Xer. Geraldine Ann Ferraro of New York earned a place in history as the first woman vice presidential candidate on a national party ticket. In Congress, Ferraro had spearheaded efforts to achieve passage of the Equal Rights Amendment in 1972 and also sponsored the Women's Economic Equity Act in 1984. Her job as chief of the Democratic platform committee helped win 1984 Democratic presidential nominee Walter Mondale's confidence.

**22.** When I was a kid the Battle of the Bulge was not a book about getting rid of the spare tire around your middle.

Mature. During World War II, on December 16, 1944, the Germans started their Ardennes offensive, which became known in the U.S. forces' journals as the Battle of the Bulge. The battle unfolded during the coldest, snowiest weather in memory in the Ardennes Forest on the German/Belgian border. It involved more than a million men: 500,000 Germans, 600,000 Americans (more than fought at Gettysburg), and 55,000 British.

**23.** I'll never forget it. I was home from school in the summer. I sat with my mom and dad and watched as tears came to Walter Cronkite's eyes as he reported Neil Armstrong walking on the moon.

Boomer. On July 20, 1969, Neil Armstrong, a U.S. astronaut, stepped off the *Eagle* lander and uttered the famous words: "One small step for [a] man, one giant leap for mankind."

**24.** I was the only kid in the apartment building to have two Cabbage Patch Kids.

Xer. In 1976 a 21-year-old art student, Xavier Roberts, rediscovered needle molding, a German technique for fabric sculpture from the early 1800s. Roberts created his first soft sculptures and called them Little People. In 1983, they were introduced as Cabbage Patch Kids. By the end of the year almost three million Cabbage Patch Kids had been "adopted"—with impatient people still waiting in lines. The Cabbage Patch Kids became the most successful new doll introduction in history, and in December 1983 they were featured on the cover of *Newsweek*.

**25.** Some members of our generation were to be referred to as "yuppies," supposedly derived from "young, upwardly mobile professionals" or "young urban professionals." Whatever. I don't think it was generally meant as a compliment.

**Boomer. The exact origin of the term is unknown and, no, it generally wasn't meant as a compliment.**

*Do you have a good addition to Generational Voices? Send it to Info@MarstonComm.com. We'll post the best submissions on the web site to share with others and for future versions of this Generational Voices exercise. Please provide as much detail as you can in your answers. We'd love to hear from you.*

# References and Suggested Readings

*Competing for Talent: Key Recruitment Strategies for Becoming an Employer of Choice*
Nancy Ahlrichs
Davies-Black Publishing, 2000
    This book comprehensively examines the processes of recruiting, hiring, and retaining top talent. The specific examples in the last chapters are good tools for any organization to adapt.

*Winning the Technology Talent War: A Manager's Guide to Recruiting and Retaining Tech Workers in a Dot-Com World*
Mary Ellen Brantley and Chris Coleman
McGraw-Hill, 2001
    This is an excellent book on how to find the right employees in a world where technology workers are often hard to pin down. The authors discuss how to read a resume to find the "gold" you need in your workplace, they give a quick and effective description of behavioral interviewing and how to apply it in an interview, and they tell you how to advertise your technology needs in a way that will appeal to your target new hires.

*Age Power: How the 21st Century Will Be Ruled by the New Old*
Ken Dychtwald, Ph.D.
Jeremy P. Tarcher/Putnam, 1999
www.agewave.com

Ken Dychtwald looks at how the U.S. population will age and how that will affect almost every aspect of society. Baby Boomers will continue to dominate the way the nation functions, but the questions Dychtwald poses are: "Are the Baby Boomers ready for their own aging, and what will they do about it? How will medicine, employment, the financial markets, and other areas be impacted?" This book is an interesting study of the way demographics will influence our nation's future, and it gives suggestions on how we might need to prepare.

*Cycles: How We Will Live, Work, and Buy*
Maddy Dychtwald
The Free Press, 2003
www.agewave.com

Maddy Dychtwald, Ken Dychtwald's wife (see preceding book, *Age Power*), focuses on the implications of longer lives on marketing products and services. As the title suggests, life as we know it may no longer be a linear path between birth and death but a cyclical process of relearning, redoing, and re-creating ourselves. Age will become less of a factor in the choices we make.

*Gen Xers after God: Helping a Generation Pursue Jesus*
Todd Hahn and David Verhaagen
Baker Books, 1998

The authors identify early on what has become obvious to many observers of Generation X—their thirst for spirituality coupled with an aversion to formalized religion. Hahn and Verhaagen discuss how to connect with Generation X, how to help them develop their spirituality, and how to "disciple" to them. The Appendix includes tools and ideas for clergy interested in exploring the authors' ideas.

*Maslow on Management*
Abraham H. Maslow
John Wiley & Sons, 1998

This is an in-depth look at the motivation of people in the workplace. Best known for his work in psychology, here Maslow tackles workplace issues, such as the primary ingredients for motivating people, what is necessary for the creation of teams, and why employees become unmotivated and "slack" (his term). He also explores the relationships between customers and salespeople. The book is packed with information and is an interesting but challenging read.

*High Fliers: Developing the Next Generation of Leaders*
Morgan W. McCall Jr.
Harvard Business School Press, 1998
www.hbsp.harvard.edu

Morgan McCall takes a good, hard look at how to develop and create an organization's leaders by taking them from their current positions of leadership and preparing them for the next level. He encourages readers to determine the skills these future leaders will need and how the current leadership must create the appropriate opportunities for them to learn these skills. The book includes self-tests and other assessments to evaluate progress.

*Generation X: The Young Adult Market*
Susan Mitchell
New Strategist Publications, 1997

Need a statistical analysis of Generation X? This is your source. It offers lots and lots of numbers. Examples: College Enrollment, Birth Ages by Mother in 1995, Healthy Eating Habits in 1994, Income Distribution of Men by Race and Hispanic Origin in 1995. This book must be good for someone doing something, but I can't fathom for whom doing what.

*Free Agent Nation: How America's New Independent Workers Are Transforming the Way We Live*
Daniel H. Pink
Warner Books, 2001
www.freeagentnation.com

Predicting the end of the "Organization Man" and the introduction of the "Dis-Organization Man," Daniel Pink puts forth a persuasive argument that the nature of today's workplace has evolved to such an extent that we've seen the end of the post–World War II workplace. The "Dis-Organization Man" is searching for workplaces that offer fulfillment, flexibility, and an enjoyable environment, to name a few requisites. And although Pink doesn't mention the generations much in his work, there is a definite synchronicity between Pink's arguments and the Generation Xers' and New Millennials' workplace demands.

*Bowling Alone: The Collapse and Revival of American Community*
Robert D. Putnam
Touchstone, 2000
www.bowlingalone.com

This book offers remarkable insight into the disintegration of social structures in the United States, one of the major reasons for this being a generational change. Putnam thoroughly devours all the information available to document how the change has occurred and uses the past (the Gilded Age and the Progressive Era) to predict what may happen in the future.

*The Ambitious Generation: America's Teenagers—Motivated but Directionless*
Barbara Schneider and David Stevenson
Yale University Press, 1999

The authors studied 7,000 teens (the New Millennials) to gather their information. Their conclusions are that while this generation has huge aspirations for themselves, they need the help and guidance of their parents, teachers, and other role models to usher them into self-sufficiency and achievement (information most parents of teens know already). Part III, "Defining Pathways," gives good guidance for helping these "motivated but directionless" teenagers along.

*Rocking the Ages: The Yankelovich Report on Generational Marketing*
J. Walker Smith and Ann S. Clurman
HarperBusiness, 1998
www.yankelovich.com

This is a superb book on segmenting your market by generations and understanding strategies for reaching each of them. The authors are the nation's leaders in this type of study, and the book is clearly written so that everyone can understand the concepts and act upon the information.

*Rules & Tools for Leaders: A Down-to-Earth Guide to Effective Managing*
Perry M. Smith
Avery Publishing Group, 1998

This is a remarkably simple guide for leadership from a former Air Force general. Smith writes from experience and includes personal stories to illustrate his points. His military background and training provide the format for the book, as exemplified by a sampling of the chapter titles: "Decentralizing and Getting Feedback," "Scheduling Your Time," and "Reaching Outward and Upward." The Appendixes are full of "checklists for busy leaders" and are all quite informative.

*13th Gen: Abort, Retry, Ignore, Fail?*
William Strauss and Neil Howe
Vintage Books, 1993

In 1993, when this book was published, the 13th Generation, a.k.a. Generation X, was just getting attention as a unique group. The word slacker was still the most descriptive term for this group. They are a notoriously negative and pessimistic generation, and this book outlines how and why they got that way. The attitudes of Generation X have changed substantially since this book's publication, but the book provides good insight into their formation.

*The Fourth Turning: What the Cycles of History Tell Us about America's Next Rendezvous with Destiny*
William Strauss and Neil Howe
Broadway Books, 1997

This is an excellent look at our nation's future with the repetition of the generations as the foundation for the authors' study. Strauss and Howe combine history with the influence of current events to create a prediction of what we can expect.

*Generations: The History of America's Future, 1584 to 2069*
William Strauss and Neil Howe
William Morrow and Company, 1991
www.lifecourse.com

Strauss and Howe identify the generational cycle in this groundbreaking book and identify commonly known members of each of the generational types—Idealist, Reactive, Civic, and Adaptive. They explain why the cycle reoccurs and predict the future of the United States based on what each of the generational types have contributed to our country's history. This is one of the pivotal books in the study of generations.

*Millennials Rising: The Next Great Generation*
William Strauss and Neil Howe
Vintage Books, 2000
www.millennialsrising.com

The authors explore the New Millennials. Strauss and Howe are largely positive about the potential for this generation, which they study as a whole, without getting into how these youngsters will function in the workplace. (The book was published prior to the New Millennials' entrance into the postcollegiate workplace.) My only consistent criticism of Strauss and Howe is that they favor this generation too much and have a difficult time being impartial since they both have children in this generation.

*Generations Apart: Xers versus Boomers versus the Elderly*
Richard D. Thau and Jay S. Heflin, editors
Prometheus Books, 1997

This book is a collection of essays by experts who analyze everything from generational conflict to a perspective on the ways generations have viewed each other throughout history. Public policy, the impending generational shift of so many Boomers into retirement, and the impact that will have on Social Security are thoroughly reviewed.

*The People Principle: A Revolutionary Redefinition of Leadership*
Ron Willingham
St. Martin's Press, 1997
www.integritysystems.com

The book provides a superb look at what motivates people and how to get more from them. Each chapter offers a self-test for personal analysis. Though not generationally focused, this book provides excellent guidance for learning about people and how to work with different personalities.

*Rewards That Drive High Performance: Success Stories from Leading Organizations*
Thomas B. Wilson
AMACOM, 1999

Though this book was written in the heady days of 1999, Thomas Wilson reviews the best policies from many of the nation's most successful and recognizable companies and explains the pay practices these companies have instituted and how they have influenced employee performance. He studies the companies' goals for their compensation plans—enhanced teamwork, talent retention, creativity, entrepreneurial drive, and other criteria—and explains how the compensation plans were created to support and enhance those goals.

*Generations at Work: Managing the Clash of Veterans, Boomers, Xers, and Nexters in Your Workplace*
Ron Zemke, Claire Raines, and Bob Filipczak
AMACOM, 2000

This book gives superb background information for all the generations—how they became who they are and how their value systems have evolved up to the present. The case studies take a good look at typical workplace scenarios. The "Advice-o-Plenty" has some good ideas, too. If you're considering reading up on generational issues, this book is a good bet.

*Generation 2K: What Parents & Others Need to Know about the Millennials*
Wendy Murray Zoba
InterVarsity Press, 1999

The author is an associate editor at *Christianity Today*, and while the title doesn't suggest it, this is a book about bringing teens to church. The analysis of the effects of the Boomers' cultural revolution on Generation X and the Millennials is plausible, especially the impact of television. And this book, like many others, describes the Millennials' desire for a spiritual life despite an aversion to formal religions.

# About the Author

Consultant, author, and speaker Cam Marston has worked with Fortune 500 companies and small businesses throughout the world to improve multigenerational relations and communications. He has appeared in the *Chicago Tribune, Philadelphia Inquirer, Charlotte Observer, New Zealand Herald, The New York Times, BusinessWeek, Entrepreneur* magazine, and *HR Management Today*. He's also been interviewed on the *Today* show and on the BBC.

Cam's programs and concepts are the result of more than ten years of extensive research and study inside businesses of all sizes and sectors. In the course of his work, he has interviewed hundreds of representatives of the various generations. Their answers are interesting—sometimes surprising—and always valuable.

Marston began his generational-focused consultancy after several years selling for Nestlé Brands Foodservice Company. While at Nestlé he discovered that he developed closer relationships with his customers when he talked to them about subjects that appealed to their value systems. He soon learned that his customers had many different values, but the values were roughly the same in each generation.

In 1996 he founded Marston Communications. Originally his clients engaged him to conduct surveys, focus groups, and research on both their customer and employee bases. Cam's results revealed significant generational differences that his clients had never recognized.

In June 1997, *Time* magazine brought Generation X and the generational differences to the forefront of American debate with the cover article "Great Xpectations." Reading it, Marston realized his findings were the same ones the article discussed. Soon afterward he gave his first presentation on generational differences in the workplace. Using the research he himself had conducted within organizations and the explosion of information on this newly identified generation appearing widely in the media, Marston began exploring generational differences in the workplace and presenting his findings across the globe.

In 2006 Marston gave more than 105 presentations. Today his clients range from small local associations to national convention audiences of more than 3,000 and to Fortune 500 senior executives in corporate boardrooms.

See below for more information on Cam Marston and Marston Communications, including:

- Speaking engagements.
- Consulting.
- Seminars.
- Products, including video training tools and audio CDs.
- How to buy bulk copies of this book.

Go to the web site at www.cammarston.com, or call, or write:

Marston Communications
P.O. Box 9687
Charlotte, NC 28299-9687
Phone: 704-374-1413
Fax: 704-374-9096
E-mail: info@marstoncomm.com

# Index